Dorothy smiled down at him. She knew how impatient he was, but she felt that he'd remember and savor every detail of this first real night of love. It was something he'd enjoy recalling in later years, of that she was certain. Sexual pleasure, she mused, always required long preliminaries before the act itself. Haste and passion were all very well in their own way, but sexual love required more than a little finesse in order that one might derive maximum pleasure from life's greatest delight.

Vivian paused and looked up at her, his eyes sparkling with anticipation. Both of Dorothy's satin-smooth legs were bare now and she knew he awaited her next welcome comand.

FORBIDDEN DELIGHTS

LOUISE BELHAVEL

MASQUERADE BOOKS, INC.
801 SECOND AVENUE
NEW YORK, N.Y. 10017

First Masquerade Edition 1991

First printing September 1991

ISBN 1-878320-81-5

Cover design by Steve Powell

Cover photograph by Lonney Smith

Manufactured in the United States of America
Published by Masquerade Books, Inc.
801 Second Avenue
New York, N.Y. 10017

CHAPTER THE FIRST

IRELAND, MAY 1911

I.

High above the cliffs and wide bays a fleet of white clouds sailed unhurriedly inland from the Atlantic, dappling the mountains, lakes and tiny fields of the Western counties with their intermittent shadows.

Crows cawed incessantly in the tall elms, skylarks sang joyously high over the ancient battlefields and ruined citadels of legendary Irish kings and their faithless queens.

Languid seals basked on the sunlit tidal flats of Ballysadare Bay and herons patiently hunted frogs and furtive eels amid the whispering reeds fringing Lough Gara, the lovely island-studded lake overlooked by Altavra House, a Georgian manor of polished white limestone sparkling in the May sunshine.

It was a brilliant late afternoon in the West of Ireland, a delicious prelude to the beautiful summer of 1911.

The two Comerford girls, Clara and Iris, were sitting on the broad green expanse of fine lawn sloping downhill to Lough Gara, the broad lake that marked the Western boundary of their adoptive family's ancestral estate.

Clara and Iris had been adopted by the Comerfords, a loving couple unable to have children of their own. Clara had been adopted as a newborn, her natural mother supposedly having borne the child out of wedlock and unwilling or unable to raise her in the terribly provincial town in which she lived.

The Comerfords had received the news of the available child with much joy. They had waited two years and were more than anxious to begin their family. When the baby was placed in their hands they took her into the splendor of their home and raised her from the very beginning as their own, making sure that she never wanted for a thing.

Some years later, the Comerfords decided Clara should have a companion—a brother or a sister. They, too, wanted another child, finding the joys of parenthood unequaled. They returned to the agency from which they had gotten their lovely Clara and were told that it would be some years before they would be able to adopt another newborn. But there was a possibility they could take in a young girl, just four years old, two years younger than Clara, who was vivacious and very loving. The Comerfords met the child and knew then that she would be the perfect addition to their family.

Iris was accepted into the fold with all the ceremony accorded a newborn, but with more respect for personal taste. They lavished on her many toys and much love, just as they had done for Clara, so that Iris would all the sooner feel an integral part of the family.

Iris, who was a joyful young girl, took to her new family from the start. In fact, in a short period of time, Clara and Iris became inseparable, having the common background of adoption and thankful that they had the good luck to be adopted by such loving parents. They came to regard one another with a great deal more fondness than natural sisters do.

Having spent some time in other parts of Ireland as guests of the families of their respective school friends, they had returned home as young ladies on the threshold of womanhood.

Iris, who was discernibly more poised and precocious than her sister had been at the same age was saying, "Elizabeth and I were talking about love and romance, Clara. Elizabeth quite startled me by saying how very enjoyable and exciting she finds it when her male friends wickedly kiss and fondle her. We were talking to each other in private, all alone in her bedroom at Westport. You know her house, of course, that tall one overlooking the wide bay and the Atlantic. When I expressed surprise, Elizabeth began telling me exactly what happens when a man and a woman take off all their clothes and 'do things,' as she called it, with one another."

"How did Elizabeth know all this?" asked Clara, quite incredulous.

"Well, when I asked her, she went on to explain how she had once hidden and watched her older cousin doing it with a young servant girl in her uncle's Dublin home. Then she told me how she later became friendly with the girl, mainly to find out what the experience felt like, I think."

"Goodness, Iris, imagine Elizabeth telling you that! What did she say next?"

"The servant girl told Elizabeth how lovely it feels, ever so much better than what she'd been used to doing with her fingers up to then. So then I whispered to Elizabeth how you'd showed me how to use a rolled sheet between my thighs and how that felt far, far more thrilling than the use of one's fingers alone."

Clara looked hard at Iris, annoyed that she had confided their secret to Elizabeth quite so readily, but unwilling to interrupt what promised to be an interesting tale.

"Elizabeth looked very interested when she heard this and replied that it would be instructive for her to have the experience of watching me demonstrate how to do it. Then she bent her head very close to mine and whispered in my ear that, in addition to being told what it felt like to be with a man, the servant girl had shared with her two really exciting secrets. Better still, she told me that she'd even tried them out and found them to be every bit as exciting as the girl had claimed.

"Well, as you can imagine, I pestered her until she conceded that she was prepared to show me the first on condition that I reciprocate by showing her how to use the rolled sheet just as you taught me. It was in my mind, of course, to try to persuade her to tell me both, but then I immediately thought it would be better to learn the first secret right away and then try to discover her second secret later on.

"So, after a minute or two, Elizabeth said very softly that she was feeling quite excited by our conversation and, since we were all alone in the house with no prospect of anyone interrupting us for at least another hour, she would show me her first secret. Without saying another word, she led me downstairs to the dining room. I watched, very puzzled, as she took her mother's silver teapot out of the glass-fronted rosewood display case, closed the doors carefully and led me upstairs to the bathroom. Once we were in the bathroom together, Elizabeth turned on the hot tap and started to test the water with her hand until she turned to me and said, 'I think it's about right now, Iris.'

"Well, Clara, I still had no idea at all what she meant, so I simply stood waiting for some sort of clue while Elizabeth locked the door and told me to get undressed."

"Good gracious, Iris. You must have been awfully excited by this time."

"I think I was still more puzzled than excited, but that soon changed. I pulled off my yellow cotton dress and peeled off my white stockings. By now I was quite sure that whatever it was that Elizabeth was going to show me was likely to be very enjoyable and interesting.

"Elizabeth undressed quickly, taking off her dress over her head so that her hair was mussed and wild around her pretty face. Then she scrambled out of her panties, just as if she were a child readying herself for her bath. It was then, when she stood before me naked, that I could see that she isn't as well-developed a girl as I am, Clara. Her breasts are only just beginning to grow. They looked like tiny little buds, like mine did when I was about eleven or twelve, even though she's fully eighteen. And the hair between her legs is only a little blond tuft, not like my dark-red bush at all."

Clara laughed aloud. She and Iris often compared their bodies with each other when alone together in the bathroom or in the large bedroom they shared.

"When Elizabeth filled the teapot with warm water and climbed into the big bathtub, I watched her very carefully. She sat back at the curved end of the bath and opened her legs as far apart as she could manage. She used her left hand to hold her little pink slit as far apart as she was able and then, as I watched, she poured warm water from the spout of the teapot right onto that pinkish ridge we both have, the thing you told me is called a clitoris."

"Oh, do go on, Iris, this is getting ever so exciting!"

"Goodness, Clara, you wouldn't have believed the effect the water had on her when she was doing this! Her face turned a pretty pink and she started breathing very, very hard. The hand she was using to hold herself open was almost trembling as she started to knead and massage the folds to either side of the opening as well as stroking her clitoris.

"It was quite like being in a languid, lovely dream, watching her do it, because she lay back with her eyes closed and panted for breath, just as though I wasn't there at all! My first thought was to try it for myself at once; but suddenly, when I felt a warmth course through my loins, a much better idea struck me. It would be much nicer for both of us, I thought, if I filled the teapot for her whenever it needed replenishing. I also thought I should pour it for her until she decided she'd had enough stimulation. I suppose I must have been hoping that she'd do the same for me when my turn eventually came. When the teapot was empty I took it gently out of her grasp and explained my idea to her; she agreed at once, evidently delighted that I'd suggested such a thing.

"Every time I filled the teapot with warm water, I held it above her and let the water cascade over her breasts, her nipples becoming more and more erect as the flow of water grew heavier. How marvelous her breasts looked glazed and dripping with water. And then I would pour some water directly onto her clitoris. The variation made her squeal with delight. Elizabeth's nipples got ever so much bigger when the water was splashing onto her clitoris and into the warm folds of her opening and the cold air was blow-ing against her breasts. By now I was rather excited myself. In next to no time, a pretty little routine began; I'd splash her clitoris while she stroked her breasts and then I'd pour the water onto her pert pink nipples while she toyed with the folds of her open slit and her erect nub. For my own part, I wanted desperately for my turn to come.

"I'd done this six or seven times before Elizabeth threw back her head and began making an odd sort of sobbing sound while at the same time heaving her hips and her bottom up and down.

"For just a moment, Clara, I was worried in case I'd somehow hurt her. But when she looked up at me with her big blue eyes shining and yet somehow vacant, I knew right away that she'd had that lovely fluttery feeling a girl can get whenever she slides a twisted sheet or towel to and fro between her legs. The sound of her bottom slapping against the wet porcelain tub worried me slightly lest anyone should have come home. Surely, I thought, they could have heard this.

"When Elizabeth had recovered her composure at last, she was ready to do the very same for me when, at that very moment, we heard the wheels of her papa's carriage on the gravel drive below the bathroom window. We scrambled into our clothes, giggling with nervous excitement. Elizabeth was just closing the door of the display cabinet in the dining room after replacing the silver teapot when her papa came into the house through the kitchen."

Clara had been listening spellbound and laughed aloud at the end of the story. Although not much older than Iris, Clara showed no signs of having ever possessed her sister's youthful loveliness.

Instead, at eighteen, Clara was tall, slender and lithe. Her long russet tresses shone and sparkled in the afternoon sunlight as she lightly tossed her head with appreciative amusement on hearing the abrupt finale of the tale.

"Iris, dear, what a marvelous afternoon you and Elizabeth had. It sounds so very enjoyable that I really must try it out as soon as I possibly can. Perhaps we can even do it together, just as you and Elizabeth did. You didn't tell me whether Elizabeth ever did the same to you in the bathroom at Westport. Did she?"

"Oh, Clara, she did it the very next afternoon and it was every bit as marvelous as I'd hoped it would be. We returned to the very same bathroom, closing and locking the door behind us. This time we undressed each other. Elizabeth turned me around as soon as the door was locked, so that my back was facing her. At first I thought that maybe she wanted to undress without me seeing. But then I felt her fingers on the nape of my neck, first spreading up into the thickness of my falling hair, sending shivers down my spine, before she began to work all those buttons free of their holes until the back of my shirt gaped open. Then she slid it forward off my shoulders, her hands warm on my bare flesh. Next she unfastened my skirt and lifted my underclothing over my head. How lovely her hands felt when they brushed my skin, once even happening across my naked breasts.

"I turned around to face her and began taking off her clothes. When we were naked we stood for a moment looking at one another. How badly I wanted to reach out and touch her breasts. I just had to touch her nipples, they looked so soft and tender. She must have guessed that I wanted to—I daresay I must have been staring at them—for in the next instant she reached for my limp hand and brought it to her breasts. Once there, I touched my finger lightly to her nipple and it felt just as I'd imagined it would... soft and pliant and warm. But when I began moving my finger in a circular motion around it, it began to grow hard, just as it had done that day in the bathtub. It grew and grew and as it did it became darker in color. Suddenly it seemed as if I had my finger upon the hardest of tiny berries. It was delightful. Elizabeth seemed to enjoy it too, for she closed her eyes for a moment before directing me to the bathtub; saying that I was about to feel the most exquisite of sensations.

"When I climbed in she instructed me to spread my legs apart, which I did. She said that maybe I'd want to play with myself in order to lift my clitoris away from its hiding place. Knowing quite well what she meant, I did so as she filled the teapot with water. I ran my fingers over my mount and separated the folds so that the pink little nub stood up dark and erect. By the time the teapot was filled, I felt all warm and trembly. Then the water hit my body. First she poured it onto my breasts. It was shocking, the feeling of water falling directly onto my breasts and nowhere else. But soon they grew used to it and my whole body began to warm even more and quiver.

"Then the water hit my mound, some dripping down over my clitoris and over my inner thighs, even dripping down under me and sliding into my bottomhole. Oh, Clara, you can't imagine! The water started falling more vigorously, Elizabeth bringing it closer and closer to my clitoris until I felt as if consciousness was slipping away from me. I closed my eyes and must have moaned, for Elizabeth said, 'Patience, dear Iris, we need a refill.' Then, on the brink of exploding, I opened my eyes to see her refilling the pot. My entire body was taut and in agony. Also, I had grown cold, against the breezy air and cold porcelain of the tub.

"I told her to hurry and soon she was back at my side, poised to begin the flow again. But she didn't for a moment. Instead she looked at my cleft. How lovely it was, she said, as she reached out her finger and touched my enlarged clitoris. Her finger sent a thousand shivers through my body. I didn't care what she did at that point. Were she to continue touching me or start probing me I surely would have exploded onto the point of her finger. But then she pulled back, saying something about fulfilling her promise to me. Then I felt the warm cascade once again. No sooner had she begun pouring the water onto me than I began to shudder, and, like her, slap my bottom up and down, even, I think, taking my fingers and inserting them into my vagina, moving them in and out and rubbing them over my wet clitoris. Truly it was exquisite.

"Afterwards Elizabeth let me in on her second secret without me even having to ask her again. Not that I can tell you her second secret, Clara, because I promised that I'd never tell anyone, ever. Not even you."

Clara shrugged, though she secretly burned to know the rest. "Iris, if I tell you what happened to me in Donegal last month, you'll be every bit as interested as I was while you were telling me about what happened to you in Westport."

"Gracious, Clara, do you mean at Belinda's family house near Killybegs?"

Clara nodded secretively. An ill-concealed smile played about her lips as she waited for Iris to respond. The response, when it came, was exactly what she had desired.

"Clara, if you really, truly promise never, ever to tell

a single soul, I will tell you the second secret, but only after you tell me about what happened in Donegal."

Clara waited a moment and then began her story. "As you know, Iris, Belinda's family estate houses a separate guest house, in which lives the widow Marie Dolan and her son George, both of whom are close family friends of Belinda's family. Belinda is the same age as me, while George is just a little younger, by several months I believe.

"Neither Belinda nor I saw very much of George for the first few days after my arrival because he was always off somewhere on one of the tenants' farms or somewhere on the estate itself, occupying himself by shooting squirrels and pigeons or exercising his pony. In fact, I'd completely forgotten about him until one afternoon when I was returning from a long walk to the village with Belinda.

"We were walking along the path that runs through the old orchard; I think we'd stopped to hear the distant mellow note of a cuckoo when—all of a sudden—Belinda put her finger to her lips and pointed silently towards the woodshed between the orchard and the stables. I suppose I must have guessed immediately that her sharp ears had heard something unusual, so I kept very still while Belinda tiptoed forward and peered through a small gap in the rough planks that made up the walls of the woodshed. Of course, Iris, I was simply dying with curiosity to know what it was that held Belinda's rapt attention so, but somehow I managed to stay rooted to the spot and completely silent until Belinda turned to smile at me very secretively."

"Whatever was it that Belinda could see, Clara?" enquired Iris, enthralled with the mysteriousness of her sister's story.

"Don't interrupt, Iris. I was just about to add that Belinda put her finger to her lips again and beckoned me to come forward as quietly as I could so that I could share her view of whatever was in the woodshed. As quietly as I possibly could, I walked forward to join her. I should tell you, Iris, that when Belinda turned to summon me, I sensed something rather odd in her manner, as though she didn't really want to see what she was able to, yet couldn't tear herself from the sight. When I was standing beside her I looked through a small horizontal gap that was level with my eyes. It took me a few seconds to focus my eyes on whatever it was Belinda had wanted me to see, and when my eyes became accustomed to the light, what I did see made me gasp aloud with astonishment. There were two boys in the woodshed, Iris. One was George, and the other was Richard Johnson, the son of the local Church of Ireland rector, whose house was about a mile away across the valley.

George and the other boy were facing one another in a shaft of bright sunlight that poured into the dark shed through a hole in the roof. At first I honestly thought my eyes were deceiving me, for both boys had lowered their flannel trousers and their underwear so that they were both naked from their waists to their ankles. I can't remember now what I had imagined men's cocks to look like before that afternoon, but I certainly know now, both because of that first afternoon and because of what happened later. Not that I'll tell you about what happened later until you've told me all about Elizabeth's second secret."

"Oh, Clara, please tell me what the boys' cocks looked like. I've often wondered and now at last I'm with someone who can really tell me. You will tell me, won't you, Clara?" Iris beseeched her sister anxiously.

Clara grinned, blushed momentarily and giggled softly.

"Oh, yes, Iris, I do most certainly know what a cock looks like...and more besides. Remember, though, that you aren't going to hear the really exciting part of my story until you've told me all about Elizabeth's really big secret, and that's a promise!"

"Clara, please don't tease me so! You know I've promised to tell you. Please tell me what the two boys' cocks looked like."

"It wasn't at all easy to see properly at first, because each boy had his fist around his own cock and the two of them were jerking their hands up and down the length of them, for all the world as though they were trying to pull their cocks off their bodies completely. That was very surprising in itself, but what was more surprising still was that I found myself getting the most curious sensation, Iris. In fact, it was the same warm, tingly feeling that I would get in my cunny when I used to watch you playing with the rolled sheet after I had showed you that marvelous little trick!

"I can tell you that I certainly felt very odd indeed, having that tingling feeling simply because I was watching those two boys playing with themselves. But what was stranger still was the curious thought that suddenly came to me just after the tingly feeling started."

"What do you mean, Clara? What did you start thinking about while you were watching the boys playing with their cocks?"

"It sounds silly to say it now, but I found myself imagining how lovely it would be if I were standing between them, holding onto their cocks and jerking them to and fro in the same way as they were doing. More curious still, Iris, I began thinking about how thrilling it would be if I were undressed, too, and George and Richard were touching my breasts and gently stroking my cunny."

"Goodness, Clara, what a marvelous thing that would have been. You're making me feel quite warm just thinking about it!"

"No sooner had that curious daydream entered my mind than George took his hand away from his cock and jutted his hips and tummy forward because, I felt sure, he wanted Richard to admire his stiff cock and what was underneath it."

"Underneath it?" echoed Iris, puzzled.

"Silly goose! You know how a stallion or a bull has a sort of bag just under and behind his cock, don't you? George and Richard each had a bag, too. It wasn't at all easy to see Richard's because he was standing more in the shade than George. Also, he had a lot more hair on his sac and around his cock so that it seemed almost to be hidden beneath it."

"Did George's cock have any hair on it?" Iris asked eagerly.

"No, silly, not on his cock. Both their cocks were quite smooth, you see. George's cock was a lovely tan color with dark blue veins visible on it; the tip of it was fatter than the shaft and a lovely dark purple color."

"Weren't you just a little frightened?"

"Goodness, no. It was all so thrillingly new. More than anything else, I wanted to touch it and play with it just as I'd seen George doing. Somehow it looked ever so sweet and pretty, with its lovely proud crest of dark blond hair as a backdrop to it."

"And could you see the other boy's cock?"

"Not at first because he was still in the shadow, but he soon moved forward and stood next to George. Nothing happened for a moment because the boys seemed content merely to stand and look at each other's cocks. They stood with their arms by their sides to get a good view. Belinda and I could see that Richard's was longer and thicker than George's even if it seemed to be somehow softer. George's stood up almost straight against his tummy like a miniature lance, while Richard's wasn't as stiff."

"Gracious, how very exciting. What happened next?"

"The very next moment, Richard reached out and pressed his fingers lightly on George's cock, pressing downwards. Then he took his hand away and back it sprang again."

"Clara, do you know that my cunny is feeling wet just hearing you tell me all this?"

"Well, wait until I've told you what happened next. Then you'll know how wet you can feel, dearest, because George tried to do the same to Richard's without much success. Richard's wasn't nearly so springy. Both boys laughed and George said something that neither Belinda nor I were able to hear. Richard's response was a nod of assent, at which George started pulling and pushing the loose skin on Richard's cock backwards and forwards, just as he'd done with his own earlier. But this time he was doing it really fiercely, so hard and fast that I felt sure he was likely to be hurting Richard. He surely couldn't have been, though, because Richard was pushing his thighs and buttocks forward to meet the rapid movements of George's hand until, suddenly, he gave a really hard push forward and—to my absolute amazement—a jet of something spurted right out of his cock, followed by a second jet, then a third."

"You don't mean he was making water, do you?" asked Iris, her brow furrowed.

"Oh no, Iris. It was quite different altogether. There wasn't very much of it at all. The way it came out was quite different, too. The first spurt must have landed two or three feet away from Richard's cock, something I thought very thrilling."

"Did Richard then do the same to George's cock, Clara?"

"He did, but not for a moment. First he looked down at his own cock, which was quite limp after its exertions. Then he reached out and grasped George's cock. His fingers went around it tightly and he began to push and pull on it just as George had done to him. This time Belinda and I were watching closely, so we were able to notice things we hadn't noticed before when George had been playing with Richard's cock.

"When George thrust his hips and tummy forward, his bottom seemed to be clenching and unclenching, the shadow of the sun falling into the depression on the side of his buttocks whenever he clenched up. We could also see the flaming red tip of his cock squeezing through Richard's fisted grip. His body leaned slightly into Richard's and his head was bent down to look upon himself being manipulated. Then George, seemingly about to lose balance, put out his arms so that his hands rested on Richard's shoulders.

"Leaning even more into Richard than before, George's knees bent and he let out a long, low moan. The we could see the successive jets of fluid catching the light so beautifully that they looked like miniature comets."

"Oh, Clara, how lovely it must have been to see it," cried Iris, clapping her hands together with glee.

"All the while we noticed that Richard's cock was jerking and growing again, so that by the time George had exploded and gone limp, Richard was fully erect. He tried then to get George to put his hand to his penis, but George hit it away and pulled up his trousers swiftly. Richard let out what sounded like a whine or a whimper and tried to get George to take his cock back into his hand, to George's visible annoyance. But just then all four of us heard Belinda's mother calling from the house to announce that our high tea was ready. We sped away as noiselessly as we had come while the two boys must have hastened to make themselves presentable.

"When Belinda and I saw them at the table a few minutes later—for George was in the habit of taking tea in the main house—neither of us said a word about what we'd seen. So the boys kept their secret in happy ignorance of our unplanned spying on them."

Clara sighed, glad to have finished her tale. She felt certain that the hint of further dramatic revelations yet to come would impel Iris to disclose Elizabeth's second secret.

For her part, Iris sat lost in quiet thought, pleased to have heard so interesting a story from her sister and curious to hear its sequel, even if the price of hearing it did violate a solemn confidence.

From the open French windows of the dining room a brass gong boomed dully. The two sisters smiled secretively at one another and walked slowly across the immaculate lawn to Altavra House.

CHAPTER THE SECOND

II.

At the dinner table the sisters learned, with no small measure of surprise, that their father, James Comerford, had announced his intention to visit Europe in the company of his elder brother, Sir Gerard.

Clara and Iris looked at each other, each trying to ascertain the other's reaction. This was a quite unprecedented course of action for their father and their adoptive uncle alike, for both were pillars of the rural community whose hours were occupied with the running of their respective estates and with public affairs of various kinds.

It was with great interest that they heard their mother's forthright voice, "Well, really, James! I certainly think it most unfair and selfish for you two men to propose to go gadding about in this manner without so much as a thought for us."

Prudence Comerford indicated her daughters with a sweep of her arm. James attempted to explain patiently, not for the first time, that a brief journey for business purposes was not to be confused with a pleasure tour. His protestations, however, were to no avail against the strident protests of his wife. Inch by inch he gave ground until, wearily, he conceded that it would be possible for himself and Gerard to spend some weeks at least of their European visit in the company of their respective families.

After some thought, Prudence, a determined woman in her forties, outlined a plan she considered highly satisfactory. The two girls, Clara and Iris, were quite old enough and sensible enough to stay alone at Altavra for a fortnight with the household and estate servants. Dorothy, her sister-in-law, and Vivian, Gerard's son by his first marriage, would remain at Dergvone, Sir Gerard's house three miles distant from Altavra. Prudence would accompany her husband and her brother-in-law to Europe and make appropriate arrangements for the accommodation of the two households in a pleasant resort to which the two men would return from time to time in order, as she explained volubly, to spend some time with their families.

After a period of roughly a fortnight or so, Dorothy would then travel to Europe in the company of Vivian, Clara and Iris.

Prudence, although the wife of a younger son—a status of which she was keenly aware—was by far the more outspoken and forceful of the two women, as well as being twenty years Dorothy's senior.

Lady Dorothy Comerford, Gerard's wife, had married into the Comerford family less than three years beforehand. Following the death of Gerard's first wife in an unfortunate hunting accident, Sir Gerard had virtually withdrawn from society, preferring to spend his days encouraging the spread of scientific agriculture in the West of Ireland and his nights attending interminable meetings, serving on rural committees and persuading the more enlightened and less selfish members of the Anglo-Irish landlord class to accept the inevitability of Irish Home Rule. Only Prudence's untiring persistence had drawn him hesitantly and infrequently into the wider world once more. Indeed, it had been Prudence who had introduced Gerard to Dorothy Aylward, the only daughter of a minor landowning family in County Fermanagh. Vivian, Gerard's son by his first marriage, was a thoughtful and artistic boy more obviously interested in natural history and botany than in the raucous and exuberant outdoor pursuits of most young men of the Anglo-Irish gentry class.

After dinner, Prudence penned a brief but comprehensive note to Dorothy, smiling to herself in the certain knowledge that Dorothy would be delighted at the prospect of several weeks of travel and sightseeing in Europe. It was with great satisfaction, then, that Prudence received Dorothy's enthusiastic reply by the hand of the groom to whom she had entrusted her missive two hours before.

"My dear Prudence," it ran, "how very sweet and clever of you to have conceived of so brilliantly satisfactory a scheme at such little notice. I must confess that I felt most aggrieved on learning of the intentions of Gerard and James earlier today, yet it would not have occurred to me to suggest so neat a plan as the one which you have so successfully persuaded James to accept. It goes without saying that Gerard was somewhat taken aback by the news of your charming *fait accompli* and only the manifest delight of both Vivian and myself persuaded him to accept your proposal with good grace. You are, my dear, quite right in assuring both our husbands that our discreet presence will in no way encumber their various worthy endeavors."

As may be imagined, the news sent both Clara and Iris into fits of utter delight. All that evening the pair eagerly discussed what clothes they ought to pack and what books they should read beforehand.

The next morning saw the two sisters seated in the wooden summerhouse at the edge of the lawn resuming their conversation of the previous day.

"Iris, you remember how yesterday you told me all about Elizabeth and how she amused herself with the silver teapot in the bathroom at Westport?"

Iris blushed prettily. She was still unaccustomed to discussing such subjects with her sister so early in the day.

"I do indeed," Iris replied after a long pause.

"Then you doubtless remember that you so deftly endeared yourself to Elizabeth that she condescended to share her second secret with you?" enquired Clara archly.

Iris had been wrestling with her conscience intermittently over the past few hours. She had promised Elizabeth that she would guard the secret with her life, yet she had also promised to disclose it to Clara.

"Clara, Elizabeth's second secret is so unlikely and so beastly that I hope you'll believe I made it all up. You must never, never, tell anyone else. Do you promise?"

Clara swore that the promise would be safe with her. Iris drew a deep breath and began.

"I'll tell you how it came about and you can judge for yourself how much I am to blame for what I permitted Elizabeth to persuade me to experience."

"Oh, Iris! Stop being such a goose and tell me. I'm sure that what I have to tell you later on is twenty times more wicked."

"No, Clara, darling. That simply isn't possible, I'm quite, quite certain of that. By the way, did you try the warm water affair for yourself in the bathroom last night?"

"I certainly meant to, Iris, but thinking about France and Italy drove it out of my head altogether."

"Well, no matter. Let's do it with each other tonight, Clara. Then you can see for yourself."

"Oh, how wonderful. Yes, let's go up to the bathroom early to wash our hair; that way we'll have lots and lots of time. Now, dear sister, tell me your supposedly awful secret before I explode with impatience!"

"It began when Elizabeth asked me, one night following dinner, to show her what I did with the towel between my legs. Up 'til then I had forgotten all about it to tell you the truth. After all, the warm water trick had been so much more satisfying. She caught me quite off guard by asking something so inherently private in what I would have sworn to be hearing distance of her parents. I must have blushed, for she laughed and told me not to worry, that she was certain no one had heard.

"At any rate, after her parents retired to bed, which they were in the habit of doing rather early, Elizabeth and I stole off to her bedroom that was on the opposite side of the house as her parents, thank goodness."

Clara sighed. Evidently Iris was going to take as long as possible setting the scene before she actually began the story. Iris was like that, so there was no point arguing.

"Elizabeth's room is beautiful. It is large with a huge canopied bed on which must be strewn a thousand pillows. At the far end of the room there are two windows that span the length of the wall, from floor to ceiling. When we entered her room she closed the door behind her and locked it. Then she went over to the windows and drew the curtains closed. She turned to face me and said that she was ready to be shown the game with the towel.

"Clara, I'm sure you'd rather not hear the rest. Are you really sure you want me to go on?"

"Iris, dear, do please stop procrastinating and tell the whole story at once. If you delay any longer I'll hold you down and tickle you until I have the whole story, I promise."

"If you really insist, Clara, I will. You must promise not to be too appalled or interrupt any more, though."

"Silly, silly goose. Tell me the story at once."

"I told her that first she had to be naked in order for it to properly work. She went right to the task of undressing herself while still facing me. She did so very slowly, as if she were mulling over the finest of details of her dress. Every now and then, while unbuttoning the pearl buttons of her cuffs, she'd glance up at me with the most wicked of smiles on her face. It was as if she knew something that I didn't know. It made me nervous and terribly excited at the same time, thinking that perhaps she had yet another new trick to show me.

"When she was naked, she stood looking at me, her eyes unwavering as if she wanted me to admire her body. And truly she has a lovely body, as I've said before. The little blonde tuft above her cunny was like spun gold in the candlelight that flickered about the room like a thousand fireflies. After finally taking her eyes from me, she stretched and pirouetted in front of the full-length mirror that was to her right.

"Then, standing in front of the mirror, she squeezed her pert little breasts together with her hands as if to make cleavage for herself that she did not otherwise possess. I was only a little embarrassed to be watching her preen before the mirror like that. I mean, I know we all do it when we are alone, don't we?"

Iris looked at Clara for confirmation. "Well, of course I do," said Clara. "But I can't imagine doing it in front of someone else. How terribly personal and private a thing it is to look at oneself naked before a mirror, and usually it leads to something that I would be entirely uncomfortable doing before another person."

Iris nodded her head in agreement and continued. "Anyway, she stood before the mirror touching her body all over. Even though I was a little embarrassed, I could not avert my eyes. For truly it was a lovely sight, watching her admiring her body thus and, too, I was beginning to feel that rush of warmth over my body and loins.

"Then she turned again to face me. She directed me to the chair in the corner over which was draped a towel, saying it was time, that she could hardly bear the delay much longer.

"I went over to get the towel. When I brought it over to her, with every intention of telling her what to do, she told me that I also must be naked. Yes, I agreed, that would probably be better. So I undressed in front of her. I did so rapidly and she told me to slow down, that she wanted to savor the sight of my body being revealed to her. While she watched me undress she touched herself.

"When I was naked, I told her that she should lie down on the bed, which she did. Then I twisted the towel and handed it to her. I told her that all she had to do was to rub it back and forth between her legs. In order to make it better for herself I suggested she prop up her buttocks on a pillow.

"Her hand reached for a pillow and she shoved it under her bottom, thrusting her mound into the air in order to rightly situate the pillow beneath her. Then she spread her legs. I could see her cunt lips glistening and spreading apart as her legs had done. It was lovely. She looked like a flower opening its petals, her outer lips spreading to reveal an inner circle of pink that spread to reveal yet another circle of deep crimson. All the while she watched me watching her.

"After I handed her the towel, she placed it between her legs and moved back and forth against it. I was getting quite hot watching her. Her eyes closed and it seemed she was being carried off to distant places.

"But then she opened her eyes and threw the towel to the side, saying that it wasn't quite as good as other things she knew of. I didn't know what she meant and said so, unafraid to sound like the innocent that I felt I was in comparison to her. She beckoned me to join her on the bed. I climbed on and sat there, sitting on one leg while my other stretched down to the floor, only the tips of my toes able to reach the ground, so high was her bed. She crawled over to me so that her face was no more than an inch from mine. She asked if I didn't want her to show me those other things.

"I said nothing and she leaned over and kissed me full on the mouth. We stayed like that, pressing our lips to one another for about a minute before she opened her mouth and pushed her tongue through my lips. While we were kissing with our tongues, a feeling that is entirely warming and exquisite, she reached out and touched me. For some reason I hadn't expected that and flinched a little. But she merely grabbed hold of me and held on to me tightly, squeezing the flesh of my arm so that I knew it was becoming red and perhaps bruised.

"By then I was growing uncomfortable in my position and so moved into the center of the bed. I was aching all over. My leg ached from having sat on it for so long, but more importantly, my cunt ached. I wanted to take the discarded towel and place it between my legs, but knew that Elizabeth had other things in mind.

"She moved over to me and instead of kissing my mouth, she leaned down to kiss my breasts. She took one fully into her mouth and sucked on it. Goodness, Clara, I can't begin to tell you what that felt like!"

Clara had been listening open-mouthed to Iris' recitation. She eagerly spoke the moment Iris paused for breath.

"Gracious, Iris. Weren't you feeling tremendously excited? I'm certain that I would have been."

"Oh, yes, I most certainly was. It felt like each time she sucked in she was sucking in my entire body, all sensation surging through my nipple and into her hot little mouth. Then she pulled away and darted her tongue lightly but forcefully over my erect nipple. That was a different, but just as thrilling, sensation altogether. As she was doing this I suddenly felt something flicker against my inner thighs and over my mound. It seemed as if it were the flame of the candle that did this, so fast and tenuous was it. And before I knew it she was pushing me backwards and bending her mouth to my cunt as she was spreading my willing legs with her hands.

"Oh, Clara, she licked the closed lips of my cunt open and stuck her tongue inside of me. One part of me was so utterly appalled and dismayed that for just a second or two I toyed with the notion of quitting the room and fleeing from the house altogether. But despite that, I was quite trembling with excitement and the thrill of the totally forbidden as I felt her tongue rapidly darting across the outer flesh of my virgin cunt.

"And when she'd stick her tongue inside and pull it out to lick all the way up to where she then would flick the tip over my clitoris...well, I can't begin to describe it. Then I felt a burning heat build up inside, starting at my knees and rising like mercury to my loins. I moaned and actually pushed her head harder onto my cunt. I moved up and down, quite unaware of the indignity of both of our positions, as her tongue went in and out of my hole.

"Skillfully, without so much as having to leave the bounty of my sex, she twisted herself around so that she was soon spreading her legs to either side of my head and lowering herself onto my face.

"I didn't know what to do exactly, but knew that if I did to her what she was doing to me, she would be more than pleased. I stuck out my tongue and as I did so, she sat right atop it so that I found an easy passage inside of her. I don't know which was moister, my tongue or her passage. And, Clara, she tasted so sweet and warm. I licked all around the edges of her folds. Then I licked her all the way from her clitoris to her bottomhole, nuzzling my face into her cunt so that my nose was buried between the space where her buttocks come together. Then she slid back down so that my tongue was once again probing her insides and playing across the enraged bud of her sex.

"And when she clamped down on me, while beginning to suck even harder on me, I began to suck as well, taking her clitoris between my teeth and trying, it seemed, to suck it right off. I sucked with my open mouth tight over her, the tip of my tongue leveraged against her clitoris. She seemed to like that.

"Then I began to feel her squirming madly on top of me, sliding her cunt back and forth on my face. As she did this I felt my own loins writhing beneath her and I started thrusting upwards so that I could manipulate my own surging pleasure over her face and warm tongue.

"I heard her moan and she stopped licking the, though she held her face pressed hard to my cunt so that all I had to do was push a little against her lips. I moaned then, because the release that was rising in my cunt had first to rise in my throat. She ground her slit open onto my mouth. I thrust my own cunt upwards, rubbing it to her nose, her tongue, her lips, anything I could. Then there was a stillness and a blackness and this incredible rush of ecstasy that just continued to surge in both of us almost until I was wishing it would stop.

"Afterwards my face and chin were covered with her juices as was her face with mine. Then we kissed again and cleaned each other with our tongues and fell back laughing."

"Goodness, imagine Elizabeth knowing all about so many forbidden delights." Clara looked thoughtful once more. It was a pity, she mused, that she had never met Elizabeth. Still, they would probably meet in the next year or two and Clara devoutly hoped that Elizabeth would be able to teach her a whole range of remarkable things. She licked her lips at the wicked thought and smiled.

"By the time I left Westport to come home there can't have been a single inch of Elizabeth that I didn't kiss or stroke or nuzzle," said Iris wistfully. "Please don't think I'm awfully wicked, Clara, because it was all such lovely fun."

Clara laughed aloud and leaned over to kiss her sister's cheek.

"Far from thinking you're wicked, my darling, I'm thinking how very lucky I am to have such a talented and experienced sister. You will show me how to do that last trick, won't you? It sounds like such fun." Clara paused for a moment before continuing, "You know, I've yet to tell you the rest of the story about what happened in Donegal. In its own way it was quite as marvellous as what you've just finished telling me."

The muffled boom of the gong sounded from the house. A startled hare, which had been grazing unobserved a stone's throw from the summerhouse, took fright at the noise and loped away through the copse of birches. The two sisters left the summerhouse and walked gracefully across the lawn to the open French windows.

To their great pleasure and surprise, their uncle awaited them in the dining room. "We are, it appears, about to be subjected to a family conference to discuss the Comerford tribe's forthcoming invasion of Europe," Sir Gerard joked.

Clara and Iris saw little of their uncle, despite the closeness of Altavra and Dergvone. More often than not, he was busy on his estate or writing articles on poultry-rearing, rather than allowing his time to be "frittered away," as he described the normal social intercourse of Anglo-Irish families in the province of Connaught.

Immediately after exchanging warm greeting and civilities with their uncle, Clara and Iris were joined by their parents and by Gerard's wife, Dorothy, accompanied by Vivian.

Clara, glowing with the unaccustomed pleasure of seeing Dorothy and Vivian for the first time in what seemed a veritable age, surmised that France and Italy would be the major subjects discussed at luncheon and, probably, for several hours thereafter.

CHAPTER THE THIRD

III.

It was not until luncheon was over and all seven members of the two households had repaired to the drawing room and were sitting at their ease that the conversation became animated and enthusiastic.

Sir Gerard, a lean man in his early forties, smiled at his sister-in-law and his nieces, of whom he was very fond, before beginning to speak.

"When James and I first discussed the subject of a visit to Europe, dear ladies, what was envisaged was merely a brief journey to examine the workings of credit unions in rural France and Northern Italy.

"Both of us play fairly active roles in the various agricultural societies here, so we proposed looking at the livestock of continental Europe with a view to importing suitable breeding stock into Ireland to act as a nucleus here in Connaught. What we particularly had in mind were the milk sheep of Lombardy and Southern France and the poultry called *poulets de Bresse* from Burgundy.

"At no time at all did we so much as mention visiting art galleries or museums, still less the spas and fashionable resorts.

"However," Sir Gerard continued, "there is no reason why Prudence should not accompany James and myself during the busiest part of our journey, as she so readily suggested."

Clara tried hard not to smile. The thought of Gerard attempting to resist Prudence's will for long was too ridiculous a picture for her to imagine.

Gerard warmed to his theme. It was quite obvious, Clara thought, that he had managed to convince himself that the idea of a European holiday had been his in the first instance.

"Because Prudence speaks both French and Italian, her presence will be of inestimable value in our dealings with cooperative societies and the like in rural France and Italy. In Italy, especially, dealings with anyone outside the major towns would be attended by the most tiresome delays and misunderstandings without the services of a full-time interpreter."

Iris caught Clara's eye. She was giggling quietly, her face half-hidden by a large edition of *Alice in Wonderland.* Clara frowned at her frivolous and easily-bored sister; Iris was prone to attacks of the giggles which sometimes lasted for hours in recurrent fits.

As best she could from her seat diagonally across the room, Clara attempted to frown Iris into seriousness, then she turned to listen to her uncle. Gerald was explaining that the itinerary originally proposed had, following Prudence's apt suggestion, been modified so that it now encompassed travel to the Gironde and the slopes of the French Pyrenees, thence to Marseilles, where Dorothy, Vivian and the two girls were to meet up with all of them. From Marseilles the seven of them would travel to Aix-les-Bains, a fashionable spa town in Savoy. Dorothy, Vivian and the two girls would remain in Aix-les-Bains while the three "explorers," as Gerard described himself, James and Prudence, would tour Savoy and the Mediterranean coastal region. Thereafter, the entire party would travel to Pavia while the "explorers" toured the great fertile basin of the Po, the great river of Northern Italy.

Vivian, his interest whetted at the prospect of a stay in Savoy, immediately suggested that his butterfly nets and sundry appurtenances would scarcely impede the party's progress while Dorothy, consulting a pair of travellers' guidebooks, announced that both Aix-les-Bains and Pavia would be thoroughly suitable venues for herself and her nieces to sketch and paint contentedly for days on end.

It was not until several hours had passed that the luncheon party disbanded and Prudence left Altavra in the carriage to pay some social calls in the immediate neighborhood.

Clara and Iris, alone once more, sprawled on the cushions of the summerhouse in the late afternoon sunshine. The deep gold rays of the slowly declining sun illuminated Lough Gara before them, transforming it into a single vast expanse of burnished copper.

Iris flicked back a straying lock of dark red hair and gazed contentedly at the heartrending enchantment of the scene before her. Abruptly, she turned to her sister and spoke softly and anxiously.

"Clara, you never told me the second part of your story about what happened in Donegal. A promise is a promise, you know. Remember, I did tell you all about what happened to me at Westport."

Clara sighed loudly and reluctantly set aside the slim volume of verse she had been reading.

"Once you've become inquisitive, there's no stopping you, is there, dear sister? Very well, all I ask is that you don't break into my story too often, otherwise I'll lose the thread of it and have to start all over again."

Iris agreed, a happy smile illuminating her pretty face.

Clara sat silently, debating within herself where best to begin. After no more than a minute or so, Clara settled herself comfortably on the blue cotton cushion and began:

"The evening after Belinda and I had watched George and the other boy playing with each other, she and I spent hours talking about what we had seen. Belinda, with a happy inspiration, used an Italian word, *spruzzo*, to describe the sudden emission of fluid from the boys' cocks. I'm certainly not clever enough to think of a better word, so that's what I, too, shall use. By the way, Belinda has a special name for her clitoris, Iris. She calls it 'the butterfly between the petals,' which I think is a clever description, don't you?"

"It's so very, very lovely and fitting yes. Do please go on with the story."

"Once Belinda was certain that I was just as interested as she was in the whole subject, she began thinking very hard about how we could watch it again, preferably without having to hide in the shadows like furtive spies. She was right, of course, because life oughtn't to be furtive or hidden at all.

"Belinda chewed her fingernails almost down to the quick trying to think of a plan with any prospect of success. At last her eyes twinkled and she grinned mischievously; I knew at once that an audacious scheme had suggested itself to her. Knowing that George was aware of my enthusiasm for sketching, she would invite him to model for us in various poses. Once he was used to being in our presence, he could be persuaded little by little to pose as a slave or a young Spartan...any role at all that required few garments. It was a pity, Belinda said, that we couldn't involve Richard as well, but George would obviously have to suffice for the time being."

Iris laughed merrily. Belinda's cunning scheme appealed to her wicked sense of humor.

"At my suggestion," Clara resumed, "we took a full bottle of sherry from the cellar up to the loft, which is where Belinda keeps all her palettes, sketchbooks and her easel. She even calls the loft her studio, even if the narrow windows set in the gables look out over moors and mountains rather than the roofs of Paris.

"The sherry would help to relax George and make him amenable to our suggestions, I thought. Belinda suggested that we ought to sketch each other so that George would see sketches of the two of us already in the loft and not be too suspicious of our suggestion that he pose for us.

"Belinda insisted that I sketch her first, so I made a pleasing charcoal and pastel drawing of her draped in a silk Kashmir shawl. I thought it quite an accomplished portrayal of her warm, determined smile and the lovely cascade of golden curls contrasting with the richness of the shawl."

"You mean rather like the sketch of Dorothy which hangs at Dergvone?"

"Exactly. After I'd finished that first sketch, I insisted on doing a more daring sketch in pastels of Belinda reclining on the chaise longue under the loft skylight with only the Kashmir shawl around her shoulders. This second sketch showed her lovely golden hair reaching to her full breasts and the pale light of a lovely Donegal day reflected softly by the rich golden floss at the junction of her thighs."

"Elizabeth was such a willing model. She sat in the

chair, positioning the shawl just right so that one side of it fell over her left breast and the other side fell quite away from her other breast, leaving her rosy nipple exposed. Then she situated her legs so that only a hint of the light hues of her cunt was exposed. She parted her lips ever so slightly and licked her finger to wet the outside flesh of her cunt so that the light could properly reflect off of it. Then she sat back and watched me intently as I studied her body.

Clara paused, reflecting on how beautiful Belinda had looked naked. Unbidden, the thought of her sister's experiences with wicked Elizabeth came to her; she thought fleetingly of how she would have delighted in parting Belinda's thighs and tickling Belinda's butterfly with her own agile tongue. Clara licked her lips, lost in a delicious reverie, before opening her eyes and resuming her story.

"When I had finished the second sketch of Belinda and had basked in her approval, she sketched me twice. The first sketch was of me fully clad, while the second depicted a much more lovely and sensual Clara than the Clara I usually feel myself to be. I sprawled languidly on the chaise, clad in only the shawl around my shoulders. My long legs were slightly apart, my 'butterfly' peeping coyly through the curling hair of my bush."

"My entire body was aware of itself as it was being painted. I could feel each part of me as if it were actually being stroked by the brush and I envied the canvas for that reason. My nipples, which were enticingly exposed, rose as Elizabeth studied them and translated her impression of them onto the canvas. They ached and I wanted so badly for Elizabeth to come over and dab just a touch of the paint onto them in order to satisfy their need to be stimulated by something other than her eyes.

"When she studied the nexus of my thighs, I felt my cunt lips—as if they were in full bloom—opening up in order to admit her eyes. I imagined that from her eyes flowed the light of the sun that hit my folds and urged them open. How badly I ached for it to be, for at least the sun would have carried with it the heat that could have warmed my flesh and eased the dull ache of my insides."

"Clara, where is that sketch of you now?" asked Iris, enchanted that so lovely and accurate a picture of Clara should exist at all, but fearful lest it ever be seen by the doubtless unamused eyes of Belinda's parents.

"Fear not, it's locked away quite safely in a trunk to which only Belinda possesses the key, Iris. Allow me to continue."

"Please do."

"The pastel sketch made me as lovely as even the most celebrated beauty of Dublin society. I remember blushing to the roots of my hair when Belinda suggested naughtily that we'd have no trouble cajoling George to pose undraped for us if we showed him her portrait of me.

"It wasn't until the next afternoon that Belinda was able to coax George into ascending with us to the loft. Of course, the first sketches we showed him were of the pair of us fully clothed. He happily accepted a full glass of sherry while he perused the paintings. To our surprise, he was readily amenable to the suggestion that we drape him in an old curtain to represent a toga. We sketched him carefully as the young Hector or Achilles or someone like that. Next, Belinda produced her trump card. Unknown to me, she had unearthed a monochrome postcard of Michelangelo's *David*. She showed it to George and suggested that he pose totally nude for us. With the sherry he'd consumed and the very agreeable way we'd spoken to him and praised him, it was plain that he felt it would have been rude to refuse.

"He took off his shirt first, for that undoubtedly is the safest course of action for a man. Then he unbuttoned his trousers and took them down to his ankles and stepped out of them. He stood before us in his undershorts for a moment before taking a deep breath and uncovering himself fully. He blushed only a little.

"With our eyes caressing his body under the pretense of studying it as form, we saw that his cock was moving ever so slightly against his inner thigh. He was in an obvious state of distress, for it was quite plainly visible that he was becoming aroused at having us look at him. The dark blond crown of hair above his small, twitching cock caught the sunlight beautifully and served to frame perfectly the object of our desire and the source of his."

"Goodness, Clara, I'm trying hard to picture it in my mind. Do you imagine that our cousin Vivian looks much the same?"

Clara giggled, her hand covering her mouth. She had wondered more than once what Vivian would look like without his clothes.

"I've thought about that myself, Iris. With any luck we'll be able to ascertain that for ourselves when we all go to Europe together. Perhaps you and I can do with Vivian what Belinda and I did with George."

"What exactly *did* you do, Clara?"

"Don't be so impatient, darling. Let me carry on with my story and you'll hear what we did quite soon enough. By prior agreement between ourselves, Belinda and I sat quite close to George, so close that he could hardly be unaware of our presence for two seconds. As I've said, George's soft little cock began, little by little, to stiffen and grow. The movement was almost imperceptible at first, but as Belinda and I sketched steadily, George's cock grew until it was almost ready to stand upright. To our delight, it began to twitch convulsively, just as though it possessed a life all its own."

"What was George doing while this was going on?" Iris interrupted.

"At first he simply pretended that it wasn't happening, but the very second he began to look embarrassed, clever Belinda gave a little gasp of feigned surprise. With sincere admiration, she dropped to her knees in front of George and asked if she might be permitted to touch it."

"Oooh, Clara! Did George let her?"

"Silly goose, he had no choice in the matter because Belinda hadn't even finished her question before she had folded her hands carefully around the shaft as if in prayer. Meanwhile, I did my best to retain my composure and carry on sketching as though nothing at all unusual was happening within four feet of me! George's eye caught mine so I winked at him to reassure him that I was in on the plot, too. It hardly seemed worthwhile to continue the pretense that I was still sketching, because the scene in front of me was changing rapidly with each passing moment. Belinda's gentle ministrations were evidently pleasing George. He was stroking her hair lovingly as she rubbed his cock, by now as stiff as a little poker, against her cheek and her long throat while I watched, quite spellbound."

"You mean you didn't do anything, Clara?" asked Iris, who had been following every word of Clara's with breathless, rapt awe.

"Remember that George is Belinda's neighbor, not mine, Iris. It seemed only fair that she should lead the way. I simply waited for Belinda's invitation. After she had been petting and caressing him for a little while, she turned her head to me and grinned lasciviously, as if to challenge me to join in. Well, I thought, I'm certainly not going to let her have the whole show to herself, even if George is her neighbor. So I knelt down beside Belinda on the soft Turkish carpet and began to stroke George's thighs and his lovely rounded bottom while Belinda's hands began to imitate the movements we'd seen the two boys making while playing with one another's cocks. George guided her hand to show her how to do it the right way, then he began to stroke our cheeks and our hair while we stroked and petted him. Eventually he grew a little bolder and slid both his hands down the fronts of our cotton frocks and experienced something I'm sure very few grown men have had the opportunity to enjoy—the pleasure of softly fondling the full breasts and erect nipples of two young girls kneeling at their feet. While Belinda caressed George's cock, I slipped a hand between his thighs and began to stroke his lovely little sac, his scrotum, with careful fingers.

"In next to no time, Iris, he shuddered convulsively and his cream leaped forth in three successive spurts, quite soaking the shoulder of Belinda's cotton frock and making all three of us laugh."

"Was that the end, Clara, or is there more to tell?"

"The best bit was the last, Iris. Wait and listen. George knelt and kissed us both, his face positively glowing with pleasure and his eyes shining. Belinda had both her arms around him as they kissed, so I was able to reach out my hand and stroke his limp, soft cock. It felt really beautiful in the palm of my hand, like a newborn kitten. The thrilling purplish-red head was a lot less ruddy now, but the sensation of actually touching a cock for the very first time was quite thrilling all the same. On a sudden impulse I bent my head and kissed it lightly, making it twitch ever so slightly."

"Gracious, Clara, you kissed it?"

"Yes, darling. What's more, I went on kissing it, too, because the tiny twitch it gave made me think that a few more kisses and cuddles were all George's soft cock needed before it reared its pretty head once more."

"Oooh, Clara. You really are daring, you know."

"Then a thought occurred to me. What Belinda had done with her hands could be done just as well in a girl's soft mouth. Scarcely knowing what I was doing, I settled down on both elbows and began gently sucking George's cock, which grew stiffer and stiffer as I sucked."

"Whatever was it like?"

"It wasn't terribly thrilling at first. There was still a drop of George's *spruzzo* at the very tip, so I licked it carefully. It tasted clean, sweet and salty all at the same time. Then I concentrated on sucking. As the shaft grew harder I tried using my mouth as Belinda had used her hand, pushing forward until my nose was tickled by the crest of curly hair above his cock, then drawing my head all the way back until only the ruby head was still in my mouth."

"What was Belinda doing while you were sucking his cock like this?"

"She and George were kissing with their tongues entwined. One of her hands was curled around George's thighs from behind, so that she was caressing his taut scrotum, while the other hand had burrowed under my frock and was fingering my moist groove very softly and gently."

"Oh, Clara, what a beautiful picture that would make!" cried Iris, her eyes open wide with delight as she imagined the scene.

"Iris, darling, we really must do the same with Vivian as soon as we possibly can. You do agree, don't you?"

"Of course I do. Listen, when Mama and Papa go away to France, we must make a practice of going over to Dergvone as often as possible to practice our French. We'll be as agreeable to Vivian as we can be and in next to no time at all we'll have him eating out of our hands. Now, Clara, do please finish the story."

"Belinda's hand was scarcely in my cunny when she touched my 'butterfly between the petals.' The shudder of delight that ran through me must have communicated itself instantly to George, because he began meeting the action of my mouth with carefully-timed thrusts of his own. Suddenly, with shocking swiftness, his sweet saltiness flooded into my mouth, squirting to the very back of my throat. I didn't quite expect it."

"Wasn't it rather disagreeable though, Clara?" Iris enquired with a hint of distaste in her voice.

"Gracious no! It was really thrilling and ever so lovely. It didn't taste bad at all. Of course, I was doing it because I wanted to do it. Indeed, I'd do it again this very moment without so much as a second thought.

"On the other hand, I think a girl being forced to do it might not like it at all. A reluctant young bride compelled to perform such an amazing feat on her wedding night might well be so shocked and dismayed that she would never want to do it ever again."

Iris thought about this for a moment before agreeing.

"There isn't a great deal left to tell. I held as much as I could of George's delicious nectar in my mouth and straightened up so that Belinda and I could kiss. George's juice soon ran down our chins as our tongues entwined."

Iris stretched and yawned. "If we say we're washing one another's hair tonight, we'll have enough time in the bathroom for me to show you how Elizabeth and I used the teapot."

Clara sighed contentedly, watching an angular heron's silhouette diminishing against the golden evening sky. When she spoke her voice was a subdued purr.

"At bedtime you could even show me how naughty Elizabeth taught you to use your pretty tongue, darling."

CHAPTER THE FOURTH

IRELAND, JUNE 1911

IV.

Her bare feet leaving silent imprints on the dewy grass, Lady Dorothy Comerford glided gracefully and unseen across the croquet lawn of Dergvone House in the pale twilight of a June dawn.

She looked upwards at the lightening sky; the last of the stars were slowly fading even as she watched.

Standing on tiptoe at the mossy stone balustrade, she could barely discern the dark slate roof of Altavra House three miles away. She lit a cigarette and drew the smoke impulsively into her lungs; smoking was something quite impermissible in Gerard's company. Perhaps that was one of the reasons she enjoyed it so, Dorothy thought with a wry smile.

Barely a week had passed since Gerard had left Ireland with James and Prudence, yet that one short week had felt like nothing less than a miraculous deliverance from Gerard's company. Dorothy shivered despite her thick velvet cloak; she felt not a little guilty to be so glad of Gerard's absence.

For the first time in more months than she dared

count she had been spared his earnest daily discourses on Irish Home Rule, the necessity of ensuring that more administrative posts were offered to Catholics, the discordant and distasteful affairs of Ulster, and all the unceasing minutiae of a conscientious landowner's life.

Perhaps a prolonged tour of Europe might change Gerard for the better, Dorothy told herself. But no sooner had this thought crossed her mind than Dorothy reflected on the depressing reality of what Gerard's tour would actually entail: meetings with men cast in his own stolid mold, worthy and porcine pig-breeders who proudly wore the insignia of the Merit Agricole for their sterling contributions to the prosperity of French agriculture. There would be tours of scientific establishments specializing in fields of endeavor about which Dorothy knew little and cared less, gala dinners with celebrated herd owners and noted writers on rural drainage.

She laughed aloud despite herself. The Europe she longed to see was the Europe of dazzling cities, magnificent theaters and opera houses, renowned concert pianists, resplendent balls and, above all, delightfully civilized society. An ironic smile appeared on her lips as she thought of the immensity of the gulf between her vision of a brilliant European tour and the familiar dull earnestness that almost certainly awaited her whenever Gerard spoke to her.

In spite of her depressed spirits, Dorothy felt pleased that she would be visiting what she had come to regard as real civilization in the company of Vivian, Clara and Iris. The presence of the three young people might turn even the most boring occasion into a lighthearted romp, she reflected happily. Her mood buoyant now, she whistled aloud a snatch of Italian opera.

A startled hare loped across the croquet lawn behind her, alarmed by the sudden noise.

Dorothy lit a second cigarette from the stub of the first. Yes, it would be good to leave Ireland and her interminable and tiresome squabbles behind, if only for a few short weeks. It annoyed her even to remember how often she had had to struggle to keep herself from screaming aloud with boredom at the very mention of Home Rule. She ran lightheartedly over the lawn and into the house, her head awhirl with visions of sophisticated pleasures.

A dream of a less earnest, more enjoyable life filled her mind as she slid once more into her soft bed.

Three miles away from the bedroom in which Lady Dorothy Comerford slumbered and dreamed, Clara and Iris lay curled asleep together.

They had spent long hours in each other's arms. It had been Clara who'd instigated the physical contact between the two. She had been the one to pull her sister to her and lay her lips upon the soft fullness of Iris' breasts. Then they had kissed before climbing eagerly into bed with one another. Clara had moved down to tease her sister's engorged nipples with her teeth and from there to taste the sweetness of which Iris had earlier spoken.

Clara found it sweet indeed. Iris, in a shudder of delight at the first touch of Clara's careful lips upon the flesh of her inner thighs and the delicacy of her tender cunt, had wrapped her legs around Clara's neck to draw her even closer into the wellspring of her pleasure.

After a few minutes she had pulled away, knowing Clara to patiently be awaiting her own pleasure.

Instead of climbing into the mutually satisfactory position, she had crawled between her sister's legs, laid herself prone on the bed and, parting Clara's cunt lips with her fingers, had taken to the task of licking her sister quite ardently. She had known just where to dart the tip of her tongue in order to elicit from a reeling Clara the deep intonations of her ecstasy. When Clara had spent on Iris' face, she returned the joy she had just received and began fingering her sister's clitoris until Iris' hands joined her own to bring her to a fully satisfactory orgasm.

So enthralled had they been by the Sapphic delights in which Iris had proven herself an adept teacher and Clara a more-than-willing pupil, that long minutes had stretched to hours; dawn had streaked the sky with the promise of a fair morning before the sisters, exhausted by one another's ardent caresses, had fallen asleep in a passionate embrace.

To the sisters, the departure of their parents in the company of Sir Gerard, their uncle, was no occasion for distress or self-pity. The staff at Altavra left them to their own devices and desires, much to the girls' delight and relief. The housekeeper thought it particularly charming that the girls chose to sleep in the same bed during their parents' absence and was pleased that the sisters visited Vivian and his stepmother at Dergvone unfailingly every afternoon.

At seven that morning Vivian finished inspecting the last of his mother's traps in the overgrown shrubbery that lay between the summerhouse and the disused barns of Dergvone House. A scant six specimens merited the distinction of painless death and painstaking preservation, but Vivian was gleeful as he closed the last trap carefully and hastened to his study and bedroom. In a few short days he would be in France; a world of new and different experiences beckoned enticingly to him, a world composed of a different language, unfamiliar tastes, smells and sounds. A contented smile wreathed his young face as he thought of his cousins' daily visits, now so regular a part of his day's routine that it seemed to him they had become a permanent fixture of his life.

For Vivian, life had become very agreeable indeed and became even more so with each passing day. Every morning was spent in adding to his growing collection of Irish lepidoptera, following which he read his science books and made copious notes in the hour or so before lunch was ready. The hours between lunch and the arrival of Clara and Iris were spent in reading the history texts he was expected to know thoroughly before being accepted as an undergraduate at Trinity College in Dublin.

He had come to relish every minute of every hour spent in the company of his cousins; together they recited French verbs and engaged in the frivolous badinage of hesitant Italian.

At first there had been awkward silences, but within a very short time this changed. One afternoon, Iris had clumsily spilled a glass of water into his lap. Apologizing profusely, she had taken her lace-frilled handkerchief to his thighs and into the space between them. Her hand, as it slowly and deliberately pressed onto his lap, had caused him to become visibly and quite unmistakably aroused. When she had seen this, she pressed all the harder and all the more pointedly, aiming to brush the bulge that had grown beneath his trousers. He had been momentarily appalled when Iris' small fist had clasped his erection through the thin white linen, but his embarrassment had been instantaneously transformed into bewildered happiness when she kissed him lightly on his parted lips and murmured a tender endearment into his red ear.

Meanwhile, Clara had tactfully averted her gaze in a successful attempt to conceal a paroxysm of stifled giggles.

Afterwards they had returned to their studies; Clara and Iris feigning an increased interest in the French language and Vivian agonizing over the throbbing sensation in his loins. His only recourse was to press down on it with his hand and wait until a more appropriate time when he could bring himself to a rapid, most needed release.

Ever since that first day, not an hour had passed without a similar incident. Emboldened by his cousins' attentions, Vivian had eventually retaliated. Clara had been facing a sandal-clad Vivian across a green card table in the conservatory when an impulse had led him to ease his foot out of its sandal. He had gradually extend his leg until his bare toes rested on the curved edge of the chair between Clara's thighs. Like a small and timid woodland animal the foot had crept forward until Clara became aware of its presence.

With consummate, unstudied aplomb she had slipped one hand below the table's concealing edge to guide the intruder to a furry haven in which an affectionate toe could romp with an altogether more sensitive organ.

At length Clara, her face an interesting shade of pink and her breathing oddly labored, had managed to say firmly to Vivian, "This little mouse has been teased quite enough for now," and had winked broadly at Iris before insisting on changing places with her.

Iris, totally mystified, had no sooner been seated than Vivian's foot had repeated its journey only to encounter an even more hospitable reception in a smaller and moister little dell. Iris all but abandoned even the pretence of reciting her verbs as Vivian's toe tickled, nudged and prodded that part of her she now referred to habitually as her 'butterfly' until the butterfly's owner breathed a sweet moan of contentment.

This game had been repeated daily for nearly a week in the warmth of the conservatory at Dergvone. On the fourth day, a pair of unseen eyes had witnessed Vivian's prolonged caress of Iris' most secret parts.

It had not been Dorothy's intention to spy on her stepson or his cousins; she had entered the far door of the conservatory in search of a letter mislaid the previous day. On seeing the letter and its accompanying envelope on the floor near the threshold, Dorothy knelt to retrieve it and, glancing obliquely through the tendrils and vines, had seen what was surely intended to have been concealed.

She felt at once startled, amused and resentful. Two minutes after her silent and unobserved departure from the conservatory she stood thinking beside the mossy stone balustrade. Lough Gara's still surface mirrored the scattering of wooded islands and the cloudless sky, but Dorothy's thoughts were not of the beauty of the scene before her. Instead, her thoughts, breathed half-aloud, were on the scene she had unintentionally witnessed.

There's no sense in being angry with the girls, Dorothy. They're both young and full of joyous energy, just like Vivian.

There's no sense in being angry with yourself, either. How could you ever tell Vivian how much you care for him? It's impossible, completely insane to even contemplate. Be sensible, for Heaven's sake. The only thing that does make sense is to talk calmly and rationally to the girls about how they may avoid the unthinkable mishap of unplanned motherhood.

Having come to this conclusion, Dorothy allowed herself to speculate on how much she would relish Vivian's ardent if inexperienced caresses, if only circumstances permitted such a thing. She became aware of a sudden warmth and dampness between her thighs, an unusual sensation for her, trapped as she was in a marriage to a worthy but undemonstrative man. She dismissed the daydream angrily, annoyed at herself for permitting her imagination to harbor forbidden thoughts so impossible to realize.

"Silly, silly girl," she murmured. "He's your stepson and you can never have him. Never. You simply can't and that's all there is to it!"

With her teeth clenched she walked into the house to resume her packing. She would be leaving in a few days, she remembered. There remained much to be done, a host of things to be left in good order before her departure with her charges. Despite her earlier annoyance with herself, Dorothy still felt more than a little resentful that the sisters, who were not so very much younger than she was and who were certainly older than she inwardly felt, were far more likely to enjoy France and Italy than was she.

She completed her packing carefully before standing in silent thought. Spurred by a sudden whim, she unearthed and packed a leather-bound diary and a plump address book.

She glanced at the bedroom clock. It would be many hours before she would be obliged to descend the staircase, a thought which greatly pleased her. She tried to remember every detail of the scene she had witnessed in the conservatory, an effort which summoned to her mind a summer's day in her past.

How many years had gone by since that turning point in her life? Nearly a decade, she thought, remembering that the war in South Africa had been thundering on the distant veldts and stony hills of the Transvaal. She had been no more than a girl on that day of remarkable extremes. She remembered how what had begun with her unavailing pleadings and tearful protestations had ended with her unchallenged possession of unimaginable power over two considerably older men. Dorothy chuckled happily at the memory of her abrupt change of fortune, inconceivable at the day's outset.

Curled languidly and luxuriously in the many-cushioned window seat of her bedroom, Dorothy could remember every subtle nuance of that day which had, at the end, brought her so much power and so much happiness.

It had happened one night following a long dinner. Two of her father's friends from his university days, whom Dorothy had known since she was a child, were staying the last few weeks of July with her family. The two men were partners, as well as friends, and were in town on business. Her father, who was in the habit of maintaining close ties with friends and acquaintances who carried with them a certain amount of importance, had insisted that they stay at the house whenever business called them to his area.

One night after dinner the two men had stayed up late in order to get some work done. They had insisted that their host and hostess, who were always quite generous with their accommodations, retire to bed as usual. They said that they could see themselves to bed when they were finished working, and that unfortunately would not be until a much later hour. They withdrew to the study, poured brandy for themselves and settled in to work.

Dorothy, who had gone to bed some time before her parents, found that she couldn't sleep. Oftentimes when she had trouble sleeping, she would read a book. After a short while, she would close her book and then her tired eyes and sleep would fall easily over her. Relighting the lamp by her bed, she realized that she had left her book in the study. Not knowing that Arthur and Edward, who had insisted since she was just ten years old that she call them by their first names, had stayed up late to work, she headed downstairs. Thinking that she would be the sole person about the house, she hadn't bothered to cover herself with her bathrobe. She went down to the study clad only in a short nightshirt.

It was not until she had turned the corner into the room that she realized her father's friends were in there and that she was quite improperly dressed. Arthur, who was sitting on the thick velvet sofa, laughed when he saw her surprised expression. He motioned for her to come sit by him on the sofa, saying that they were old friends and that there was nothing about which to be embarrassed. Not wanting to be rude, and having always liked the men, particularly Arthur, she sat down. When she did, she pulled her nightshirt as far down over her bare thighs as was possible without causing a large gap at the neck of the shirt, down which could be seen her full, rounded breasts. She pulled her legs close to one another and sat on her hands, not knowing quite what to do, but knowing that if her father or mother were to see her sitting there, dressed as scantily as she was, they would be appalled.

Still, Dorothy couldn't help but recall how many times she'd dreamt of these men…thoughts that were unquestionably improper for a young lady. Both men, particularly Arthur, were well built and handsome. They exuded, to Dorothy, masculine strength, and since she had been a girl, they had always flirted harmlessly with her, causing her to think about them in funny ways when she was in bed at night.

Coming out of her brief reverie, she became acutely aware of Edward, who sat across from her in a cracked leather armchair. He was looking at her thighs. When she would catch him, wishing she hadn't, he would look away as if embarrassed. It was strange to her that he, a grown man, should seem so awkward. But he couldn't help but glance, whenever possible, at her long legs. Arthur sipped his drink and questioned Dorothy about school and her upcoming plans for university, the entire time letting his eyes roam over her body.

Despite herself, Dorothy felt a tingling sensation that began in the back of her knees and soon spread upwards to her loins. It was strange and wicked, but it actually excited her to be looked at and so obviously admired by these two older men. She leaned back on the sofa, taking her hands out from under her so that she had to wiggle her body a little in order to free them. Her nightshirt had ridden up further on her legs when she had leaned back, exposing a greater amount of the bare flesh of her milky white thighs. Both men acknowledged this exposure with approving, if not lascivious, looks.

Edward asked Dorothy if she would like some brandy, saying that he thought she was quite old enough to have a sip or two and that if she were having trouble sleeping, for she had confessed as much as soon as she had seen them in the study, it would make sleep come more readily. She said that she would like some and Edward rose to pour her a glass, turning as soon as he was standing so that neither she nor Arthur would notice the swelling between his legs. When he handed it to her, she laid her delicate fingers lightly over his before grasping the glass and pulling it toward her. She brought it to her full lips and slowly let the liquid pour into her mouth. The brandy ignited Dorothy as it slid down her throat and it felt as if her entire body blushed a deep crimson. In order to recover herself she took another sip of the liquid. Warmth rushed through her veins.

Edward sat down while Arthur continued to talk to her, telling her some story to which she didn't listen and about which he didn't care. He hadn't remembered when she had grown into the young woman who was seated beside him. He had always thought of her merely as his friend's daughter and little else. If he had flirted with her it was because he flirted with everyone, not because she stood out in his mind as the lovely creature she had evidently become.

Feeling warmed by the drink and excited by the men's eyes upon her legs, she giggled and parted her thighs slightly, slowly. Beneath her nightshirt she was naked. She tilted her head back and closed her eyes, feeling the air coming up under her moist cunt. The shirt had ridden to the top of her thighs. That she had spread her legs, however slightly, escaped neither Arthur nor Edward, though the latter was in a better position to see what was being offered to his eyes.

Dorothy, with her eyes closed, felt the tension growing in the room, and knew that they were looking at her. She sprawled against the sofa, feeling the soft velvet beneath her thighs, the cushion coming up under the weight of her body and the brandy warming her blood and muscles. She still didn't open her eyes as she spread her legs even wider apart. This time the nightshirt came up to half-expose the blond floss of her cunt. When finally she opened her eyes, she saw Edward sitting still in his chair, no longer bothering to politely avert his gaze that rested wholly on her upper thighs and the space between them. She could see that he had his brandy glass placed on the plainly visible bulge in his lap and that he was pressing down on the glass in order to press down on his cock. Arthur no longer spoke.

Feeling an ever increasing void in her cunt, Dorothy set her glass down and lifted her nightshirt over her head. The men smiled and didn't protest, even though she was the daughter of one of their closest friends. Her breasts, they could see, were full and well rounded, though not entirely grown. Her nipples stood out an inch, it seemed, from the white hillocks on which they perched. Dorothy parted her legs even more and touched her breasts. Edward could see, gleaming in the light, the wetness that now seeped from the open mouth of her cunt and glazed its lips.

Arthur took his cock out of his pants, a move that startled Dorothy. It was long and hard, and of a much richer color than his skin. Edward merely sat with the glass pressing into his lap. Then Arthur moved closer to Dorothy who, despite her gestures, hadn't expected to be touched by them. Arthur reached out and grabbed her thigh. He squeezed it until she yelped softly. Then he reached his hand up to her breast and touched her nipples before cupping the whole of her breast in his rough palm. Dorothy was shocked but couldn't help but notice the feeling that fluttered through her as he pressed her breast harder. All the while, Edward sat watching.

Next Arthur took her hand and set it upon his cock, wrapping her fingers around the shaft as if she had no will of her own.

His cock sprang from his trousers, Dorothy recalled having thought at the time, like the slender pistil of an orchid.

He placed his hand over hers and squeezed so that she was fisting his cock as hard as he would have done it himself. When he loosened his grip, Dorothy pulled away and stood up. The pleasure, though still lingering in her loins, was all but gone. She had enjoyed sitting there, exposing herself to the appreciating looks of these men. But when Arthur began to get insistent and a little rough, she grew frightened.

Standing up, she went to pour herself another drink. As she stood at the table, she heard someone coming up behind her. She guessed that it was Arthur, for Edward had made no effort to touch her. Then she felt a hand spreading her buttocks apart. She gasped. Another hand inserted itself between her thighs and pushed them apart, only brushing against the surface of her cunt. She stood spread-legged with her back to the assault, afraid to move. Then she heard the rustling sound of fabric and felt hot flesh meet her own, touching the space of her spread buttocks. She felt something slide between her thighs and touch the damp flesh of her cunt.

In spite of her fear the feeling of the burning hot flesh pressing to her most intimate treasure was pleasing. She could feel herself becoming wet and aroused. Two hands grabbed her hips and pulled her back so that her buttocks hit against the other's body. Without having time to think about it, she felt the tentative penetration of the man's cock into the outermost folds of her virgin cunt. Then, being pulled back still more, she was penetrated fully, the entire length of the cock thrusting hard into her while two hands reached around to grab and squeeze her breasts. She gasped and struggled for breath, turning her head slightly.

Pounding into her was not Arthur, but Edward, who obviously could no longer bear the pulsating agony in his cock. Looking at her subtly curved backside had only increased his desire and so he had risen to have her. He knew it was wrong, but he was no longer in full control of his actions.

Now it was Arthur who watched, amused and aroused by the sight of Edward pushing into her and further aroused by the sound their flesh made as it came in contact and rubbed the shaft of his cock up and down with one hand while squeezing the reddened tip of it with the other. Then he saw Edward ram her hard, his buttocks contracting with the force of his thrust, freezing there in his surging release. Edward's head fell against the back of Dorothy's neck and Dorothy felt him shoot something inside her. Then Edward let go of her and pulled his dripping, softening penis out and let it drop against his inner thigh.

In spite of her initial outrage and anger at having been thus assaulted from behind, Dorothy had rapidly come to feel her body responding. Her despair had given way to sensual delight just before Edward had stiffened and released his load inside her slit. Her senses were now heightened and her body ached. She had been close to orgasm, of that she was certain. Even the pain of initial penetration had been forgotten.

She went over to Arthur who sat fondling himself more calmly now. She climbed on top of him, straddling his legs, and slid down over his upthrust cock. There she manipulated her body over his, rubbing her enlarged clitoris against the base of his thick tool. Soon the intense pleasure that she had come close to feeling with Edward mounted again. Arthur, who felt his own pleasure increasing, tried desperately to lift her up so that her cunt would ride up on his cock and then slide back down over the length of it. After years of many varied sexual experiences, he knew this was what pleased him the most in the end. But Dorothy was in the midst of her orgasm, which was strong and flowing through her, and could not be raised from the spot at the base of his cock upon which she was impaled. After the spasms subsided she climbed nimbly from Arthur's lap, leaving him unfulfilled.

Arthur's cock was dripping with Dorothy's release and probably Edward's, too. It ached and he called Dorothy back, but she would not come. Suddenly she realized the power inherent in the situation. Instead she lowered herself to the floor and ordered him to suck her. She instructed him to lick her cunt thoroughly, until there was not a trace of fluid on it, and then, and only then, would she do the same for him.

Meanwhile Edward had grown hard again. With Arthur scrambling into position, Edward stood erect before them. Dorothy told him to get down on his knees and fondle her breasts. She was delighted when he did. With Arthur sucking and licking her cunt, and Edward fondling her breasts with one hand and his cock with the other, Dorothy was pleased beyond expectation. As she felt her second orgasm rise in her body, she thrust upwards so that she was able to rub her cunt against Arthur's face. She clamped her hand over Edward's on her breast in order to have him squeeze harder. It seemed to Dorothy that the harder her breast was squeezed the more intense the sensation that surged through her.

When she was finished she told Arthur and Edward to sit next to one another on the sofa. She took Arthur's cock into her mouth, wrapping her lips tightly around it, and sucked on it, while she manipulated Edward's longer but more slender cock with her hand. Then she reversed positions, so that she took Edward's cock, which was sweeter tasting, into her mouth, and Arthur's into her hand. When Arthur's release began to rise to the surface, he pushed away her hand and pulled her head down and her mouth onto his cock. Dorothy nearly choked as his salty flood streamed down her throat. Edward began to grow increasingly excited. He quickly got down on the floor, kneeling behind Dorothy, and pushed his cock into her cunt as he had before. He began to come immediately as Arthur continued to pump into her mouth. With Edward pulling down on her hips to have her sit on the base of his cock, Arthur pushed down on her head and pushed his own hips upwards. She felt as if their two pricks would meet somewhere in the middle of her body, so far down her throat had Arthur's penetrated and so far up into her womb had Edward's climbed.

Blushing slightly at the memory, Dorothy delighted in the recollection of the sight of Arthur's nose snuffling in the richly curling undergrowth of her fragrant pussy while his unseen tongue labored lovingly and deliciously over the tiny dark-hued ridge that most craved its attention.

She lit a cigarette and slowly exhaled the fragrant smoke of her Turkish cigarette.

"Would the future ever be as thrilling and delightful as the past now appeared in retrospect? The prospects seemed doubtful indeed, but Dorothy resisted the gloom of depression that threatened to engulf her by turning her thoughts to Vivian.

Perhaps, just perhaps, it would be possible after all. Not here at Dergvone, of course, but perhaps in France or Italy the chance would come.

She panted aloud as her slender fingers slid beneath her skirt and between her thighs and caressed her hooded clitoris, as her imagination caressed Vivian's slim body.

CHAPTER THE FIFTH
LONDON, JUNE 1911

V.

Dorothy's travel guide to the Mediterranean informed her succinctly that travellers from Britain to Marseilles, the great French port of the Mediterranean Sea, might travel by the P. & O. Express starting on Thursdays from London, or by the Calais-Mediterranean Express, or even by one of the many ordinary expresses from the Channel ports of France.

Her enquiries at the offices of the enticingly named International Sleeping Car Company in Cockspur Street had satisfied her that the party's journey to rendezvous with Gerard, James and Prudence was to be as expeditious and as luxuriantly comfortable as possible. Accordingly, she had booked reservations for herself, Vivian, Clara and Iris on a convenient train and the tickets lay safely immured in her carryall. At her insistence, she and her young charges were spending two nights in London, the throbbing heart of the British Empire.

"How very dowdy and very provincial we must seem to the other guests in the hotel, Dorothy," Clara had confided shortly after their arrival.

Clara's tactless yet innocent remark had brought an involuntary blush to Dorothy's cheeks and she had had to concentrate hard to keep her voice even as she replied, "True, Clara, very true. How remarkably clever of you to have noticed something so glaringly obvious. We are merely birds of passage here, not true inhabitants of this great metropolis. It may well happen that you will find yourself living in a great capital soon enough. Our outlandish accents and Vivian's colossal Alpine boots are quite enough to make it clear that we are merely minor Anglo-Irish gentry, a class of person doomed to disappear as completely as the dinosaurs! Perhaps the hotel will decide to charge a small fee to the general public in order that large numbers of people might have the opportunity of feasting their eyes on such rarities. Would you rather enjoy that?"

Iris and Clara giggled awkwardly at Dorothy's curious retort. It was difficult for them to understand her more cryptic utterances sometimes, utterances that seemed to have become more and more strange as they made their journey from Boyle to Kingstown abroad a slow train. When they had finally arrived in London they were travel-weary but thrilled.

Now the trio sat in the palm court of the hotel, the sumptuously vulgar apogee of Edwardian luxury. A neat stack of the most recent travel guides to Southern France, Northern Italy and the Mediterranean were at Dorothy's right hand, evidence of her industry earlier in the day.

Vivian had earlier disappeared in order to obtain additional devices with which to trap, kill and mount butterflies and moths, much to Dorothy's pleasurable, if ironic, approval.

"I simply can't imagine what James will make of your incessant persecution of those poor insects,

Vivian," she had said. "In all likelihood, he'll take you aside quietly and tell you it isn't 'the proper thing,' unlike the noble mass slaughter of hand-reared pheasants he loves so!

"Still, if you need yet more equipment to aid you in your efforts, you'd certainly be well advised to buy it in London, for I suspect Aix-les-Bains will be as ill-provided with purveyors of lepidopterists' devices as Boyle or Sligo."

Dorothy sipped her scalding tea cautiously and watched Clara leaf through the guidebooks before tossing them aside in favor of the more exciting Guide to the Mediterranean. Iris, who had a certain wistful look about her, contentedly stared in provincial awe at the bustle of people around her. Looking up, she caught Dorothy staring at her.

"Iris, there's something we must discuss. You are included, Clara, my dear. Perhaps we ought to go upstairs and have a long chat, the three of us, because it concerns the sort of matter young women of our class are seldom given to discussing in public."

Mystified, the two sisters followed Dorothy to her room and sat side by side on the mock-Regency sofa facing her.

"I scarcely know best where to begin, my dears, so I shall begin at the beginning and say what I have to say. Naturally, this conversation must not reach the ears of Vivian. I'm quite, quite certain that I can rely on the discretion of you both. I can, can't I?"

The sisters nodded in assent. This was a Dorothy they had never seen before, a rather intimidating and self-possessed Dorothy. They listened raptly for her to begin.

"I want to talk to you about how young women, young women like yourselves, may enjoy life to the fullest without the constant lurking terror that motherhood will suddenly be thrust upon them as the consequence of a single indiscretion."

Clara's lovely face turned a deep crimson and Iris stared open-mouthed at Dorothy, eager to know what she was about to say next.

"You certainly blush very prettily, Iris. As you hardly need to be told, I am older than either of you, judged by calendar years. As fortune would have it, my knowledge of these matters is far greater than yours, as is my discretion. Discretion is something a woman must cultivate, for women like us cannot afford to lose our reputations due to carelessness. Before I go on, I must tell you something which will immediately lead you both to think the very worst of me; I happened to see you girls and Vivian together in the conservatory at Dergvone and if what I saw is any guide at all, in next to no time one or the other of you—possibly both of you—will have Vivian's sweet cock inside you."

"You were watching us in the conservatory, Dorothy?" cried Clara incredulously, feeling most dreadfully betrayed. Iris blushed deeply and looked at the floor.

"It was, I assure you, quite unintentional, Clara. It rather hurts me that you seem to be willing to believe I deliberately spied on you. All the same, Clara, I confess myself very glad that I saw what I did see in the conservatory, otherwise it would not have occurred to me to talk to you girls about something very, very important.

"You must see, both you girls, how very unfortunate it would be for either of you to find yourselves wanting to fully reciprocate Vivian's affections, but terrified to do so for fear of consequences too appalling to contemplate."

Clara, who had been listening intently, looked

Dorothy in the eye and spoke. "Dorothy, please forgive me for believing the worst of you, even if it was only for a moment. I really didn't mean what I said at all. I'm so sorry."

"Well then, let's all share a bottle of champagne, shall we? There's a lot to be said before Vivian returns with his spoils and his long eyelashes."

The sisters laughed happily, but it wasn't until the iced champagne, summoned by telephone, arrived that a blushing Iris spoke for the first time.

"Dorothy, are you really going to tell us how one might, might…"

"*Fuck*, Iris?" enquired Dorothy lightly.

Iris blushed more deeply this time, quite astonished to hear such a word from Dorothy's lips, before nodding rapidly.

"Yes, Iris. That's exactly why we are having this intimate little tête-à-tête.

"It is imperative, in my view, that both of you should know these things quite thoroughly before you find yourselves in Vivian's company for days and weeks on end. It is, you see, quite possible for we girls to have as much pleasure as we like without the slightest fear of the consequences."

"Oh, Dorothy! How wonderful of you to be so sweet," Iris responded, her eyes shining.

"Dorothy, do you really, really mean it?" asked Clara quietly.

"Of course I do, you silly goose. Now, listen carefully. We don't really have a great deal of time and in the next hour or so there's a great deal I must tell you and show you. First of all, let me show you something I always use after I've been fucking." As Clara and Iris watched open-mouthed, as amazed to hear Dorothy use such language as they were intrigued by what was coming next,

Dorothy produced an object she carefully informed them was a rubber douche and held it aloft before passing it to Clara.

"Goodness, Dorothy. It's almost the same as a hot water bottle turned into a snake."

She passed it to Iris, who ran her fingers curiously over the bulging bulb and the smooth black nozzle at the end of the object's serpentine neck.

The two sisters sat silent and fascinated while Dorothy swiftly and calmly removed her clothing after reassuring herself that the door to the corridor was secured.

Dorothy paused, her hands on her hips, and turned slowly around as the girls stared.

"Well, look at me now, Clara. Undressed I'm hardly a day older than you, am I?"

At twenty-three, Dorothy's tall body was that of a mature and radiantly beautiful woman at a woman's loveliest age, thought Clara with a sudden pang of envy.

Her breasts were full but perfectly symmetrical and delicately shaped, the nipples an enchanting rose-pink. Dorothy's stomach was flat, smooth and unflawed; as the girls looked on, she traced its smoothness with delicate fingertips. Her back, long and narrow, reminded Iris of a painting of Diana the huntress. The perfect curve of the pale cheeks of her bottom accentuated her lovely long legs to perfection and her exquisitely-defined triangle of lustrous golden curls took Clara's breath away with its beauty.

The two sisters stared at Dorothy wide-eyed, lost in admiration.

Gratified by their appreciation of her charms, Dorothy smiled as she sat down in a chair and opened her legs wide, displaying without shame her pinkest and most secret parts to the girls.

She displayed the use of the douche with meticulous care. She spread her legs even wider, lifting her thighs off the chair so that her toes were pointed on the floor in support of her, and touched the tip of it to the warm lips of her cunt. She said how nice and cold it felt to her flesh before pushing it inside of her. The girls watched as it disappeared behind the pink folds of her opening. She wiggled her bottom just a little before pulling it out, explaining precisely how and why it was used. Satisfied that they had understood everything she had told them, Dorothy lit a delicately-perfumed Turkish cigarette and took a long sip of champagne before speaking.

"Look, girls, I trim my bush with nail scissors. That way my little clitoris isn't lost amid the curls. Not that dear Gerard would ever notice such a thing, of course, but one must strive for maximum effect, don't you think? Do you find it pleasing?"

"Oh, Dorothy, how lovely you look," cried Iris with glee and admiration. Clara echoed her sister with ready assent, resolving that she and Iris would do the same that very evening.

"I tried trimming it so that it was exactly heart-shaped when I was about your age, Clara, but it really needs the assistance of another person." Dorothy grinned broadly, then added, "Perhaps you two girls might try doing it with one another."

The two sisters giggled in unison. That sounded like so much fun to them both and they assured Dorothy that they would start to do it before bedtime. Dorothy glanced at her watch and spoke once more.

"There's another sort of douche, one with a kind of cylinder rather than a rubber bulb. One seldom sees them outside the more civilized parts of continental Europe. Somehow I doubt we'll see any at all in the sort of circles in which we'll be moving, unless we have the good fortune to make some interesting friends."

Clara and Iris giggled again, doubting the probability of such a prospect.

"Unless you have a basin or a collapsible bath conveniently at hand, it's better to use a douche in the bathroom rather than in the bedroom. Now, to be really safe, you should always have a rubber diaphragm securely in place inside your cunt."

"Where can one buy such an article?" asked Clara.

"I shall make certain that you girls are provided with at least two apiece before we leave London, my pets," Dorothy replied. "In older societies than ours, women use a remarkable array of other devices to prevent conception. I believe the Chinese used to use powdered fern seed, the Arab women employ a plug of wool soaked in the juice of the weeping willow, while our gracious and civilized Persian sisters line their most sensitive parts with the white membranes of the rind of a pomegranate."

Clara interrupted Dorothy impulsively, "The courtesans of ancient Athens must have used something, too, mustn't they have, Dorothy?"

"I seem to remember that they used to rely on a technique involving the insertion of small pieces of a kind of sponge soaked in olive oil.

"Naturally, if a man wears something to stop his sperm entering a woman in the first place, everything becomes much easier. Casanova, the Italian lover, employed a sheep bladder tied neatly in place with a colored ribbon. These days there are devices called condoms made of very thin, strong rubber of the very finest kind. An Irish doctor in the Indian army invented them, I believe. Perhaps it would be a prudent step if I obtained a few dozen of them for master Vivian if you girls are likely to be spending some time with him kissing and cuddling."

Clara and Iris blushed, tittering softly at Dorothy's remark. Suddenly grave, Clara said, "There's one thing you haven't mentioned at all, Dorothy. If we lose our virginity, we can't restore it, can we? Can't a future husband detect that a girl is no longer a virgin?"

As she looked into Clara's anxious young eyes, Dorothy was unable to stifle a laugh which had risen irrepressibly in her throat.

"Goodness gracious, Clara. If you do have the bad fortune to marry a man prepared to doubt your value because he suspects you of having known love before he entered your life, there are many, many things you can do.

"First of all, a good piece of acting on your part would be a great help; if you were to behave and talk like a shy, apprehensive little virgin, he'd almost certainly assume that you actually were one.

"Secondly, I'm sure that a girl who put her mind to it could simulate the most excruciating agony as her newly-married husband's cock pushed into her for the first time. You could manage a howl of violated pain readily enough, I think, couldn't you, Clara?"

Clara cheerfully replied that she could. Then she furrowed her brow and added in an anxious tone, "Isn't a girl supposed to bleed copiously and be, well, awfully tight, Dorothy?"

"Goodness, Clara! This has been bothering you a lot, hasn't it? Let me set your mind at rest right away; we are girls who practically grew up in the saddle. Men from our own kind of background don't really expect us to be dreadfully tight or liable to bleed. You see, all that bumping and chafing on a saddle seems to wear one's maidenhead quite away.

"As for bleeding, I believe there's a neat little trick well-known on the Barbary Coast which involves using chicken blood in a fish bladder. A bride-to-be could pass many a happy hour experimenting with such a device, don't you think?" All three young women laughed aloud at the ludicrous picture Dorothy had conjured.

Clara managed to find her voice and speak. "Dorothy, you really are a wonderful person for Iris and I to have as a friend, you know. I honestly feared that you were going to be terribly upset about what's been going on between us and Vivian, but you haven't been horrid at all. This is the loveliest afternoon we've ever spent together!"

"That was lovely of you to tell me that, Clara. So now we three girls are friends again, I hope. There is one thing that still must be done for me to feel absolutely at ease before Vivian returns."

Clara and Iris listened to Dorothy as she dressed slowly and with precise, meticulous care.

"I want both of you to pull up your skirts and show me that you both understand how to use this douche properly. Seeing is believing, you know!"

Blushing furiously despite their giggles, Clara and Iris did as Dorothy had told them. Seated side by side on the richly-upholstered sofa, their stockinged feet resting on the low table, they spread their youthful thighs wide and displayed a virtuosity with the dull red serpentine article that pleased Dorothy no less than the sight of their glossy curls.

First Iris took the instrument and, bending her head down slightly to see what she was doing, spread her cunt lips with her fingers. She pushed the douche as far into her as it would go before hitting the wall that blocked the rest of the path. Then she pulled it slowly out, enjoying ever so much the feeling as it slid along the inside of her wet tunnel. It came out glazed a milky white.

Clara snatched it from her hand, spread her own lips and pushed the coated instrument into herself. Iris sighed, knowing how it felt. Dorothy merely looked on, intent on seeing that the girls used it properly. She, too, however, could not help but imagine how it felt to the girl.

When Clara withdrew it, Dorothy took it from her and said, in order to cover up her mounting excitement at having watched the two girls inserting the cock-like instrument into their virgin treasures, "My goodness, you are luxuriantly flossed girls, aren't you both? My own little bush was nowhere near as profusely furred as yours when I was your age.

"A little ladylike trimming would most certainly be in order, I think!"

Having satisfied Dorothy concerning their proficient application of the flexible red novelty, the girls rearranged their clothes and settled down in a more accustomed posture.

Clara poured out the last of the champagne and was delighted to observe Dorothy lift the telephone and order a second.

Iris yawned and stretched before standing up and exclaiming, "Abstinence sows sand all over the ruddy limbs and flaming hair, but desire gratified plants fruits of life and beauty there."

Clara and Dorothy were enchanted, looking enquiringly at Iris until she added, "It was something I remembered suddenly from one of William Blake's poems. It seemed to be rather apt for the occasion when you said how furry we are, Dorothy."

Clara murmured softly, "Dorothy, how on earth do you know so much about this sort of thing? I'd wager every guinea in my purse that Mama has never heard of sponges soaked in olive oil or anything of the kind. For that matter, I simply can't imagine many of Mama's friends knowing anything much, either."

"You might well be very wrong there, little goose. We women are very good at keeping secrets we really want to keep safe, as I'm sure you know. Even I have my secrets, as you doubtless readily believe. But I am telling you now that a woman can find out anything she wants to know if she tries hard enough and subtly enough.

"What's more, any woman can wind a man around her little finger if she has the sense to go about it in the right way. Talking of secrets and due discretion reminds me that I have still to insist that this conversation and everything else should remain a secret between the three of us. Not even Vivian is to know, if you please. You may leave Vivian to me; until I tell you that he's had a chat from me about these things, you are most certainly not to discuss anything of the kind with him.

"It isn't that I wish to bully or obstruct either of you, but some things must be done in the proper order or confusion and disgrace will be the inevitable result, my dears."

The champagne arrived and was opened and poured before Iris, who had been thinking carefully for some minutes, spoke, "Dorothy, I'm still young. Surely it would hurt me dreadfully to be fucked. I play with myself, of course, but that's different. Please tell me the truth."

"Why should it hurt you more now than at twenty-four or thirty-four, Iris? Any girl who is old enough to bleed once a month is surely old enough to fuck, doesn't that stand to reason? What can hurt is the way one is fucked, whether it happens to be the first time or the ninety-first. When the majority of girls lose their virginity they are shy, nervous and quite overawed with it all. The shyness and the nervousness mean that their cunnies are unlikely to be moist, open and welcoming. You girls know, I'm sure, how a girl who is warm and excited opens like a flower on a May morning. Well, a girl whose cunt is tight and dry finds herself being forced upon by her bridegroom's stiff cock. It never happened to me, I'm pleased to say, but there are women I know to whom it happened on their wedding night and they still shudder and wince at the memory."

Dorothy stood up and replenished the champagne glasses of the pair. "Iris, please stop looking so anxious; we may say with absolute certainty that you will neither be a virgin on your wedding night, nor will you be likely to feel even the tiniest pain when Vivian first makes love to you." It was a considerate thing to say and it brought a pink glow to the girls' cheeks.

A discreet knock was audible at the outer door. Dorothy leaped to her feet, instantly recognizing Vivian's manner of tapping.

Without haste, she tidied away the douche and, her voice low, said, "Remember, you two, not so much as a word to Vivian about any of this," before unlocking the door and welcoming her stepson into the room.

CHAPTER THE SIXTH

CROSSING THE ENGLISH CHANNEL, JUNE 1911

VI.

“I have telegraphed ahead to Gerard and James to tell them when to meet us at the St. Charles station in Marseilles,” Dorothy confided to Clara and Vivian as they stood beside her on the upper boat deck to watch the white chalk cliffs of the English coast recede in the distance. The trio chatted awhile before Clara went below to join sleepy Iris in the cabin Dorothy had thoughtfully reserved.

Despite the warmth and brilliant clarity of the day, Vivian appeared preoccupied and ill at ease to Dorothy and at length she took it upon herself to ask him what was amiss.

“It may sound awfully silly, Dorothy, but I was just wondering how likely it is that a European war will begin quite soon. Possibly this year, possibly next year or the one after; it isn’t that I’m a convinced pacifist or anything of the sort, but I feel certain that the French will contrive to make sure that the British Empire is involved as an ally against Germany and that practically guarantees that the war will last until one side or the other is simply too exhausted to fight any longer." He stopped talking and looked Dorothy in the face, his young brow furrowed anxiously.

"Vivian, do you imagine that simply because I'm a woman I'm unaware of these things?" responded Dorothy, her voice trembling. Vivian looked hurt to be addressed in such tones and, on seeing this, Dorothy immediately added, "If it were my decision, Vivian, I'd make quite certain that you and the girls were well away from any danger of being caught up in the organized hysteria which will, I'm sure, be employed to make sure that the Empire is tricked into supporting the French if and when war does come.

"You are probably quite right in thinking that there will be a European war shortly, Vivian. We can only guess where and when it will begin. Perhaps it will be over some squalid little province of the Balkans, or over Morocco, or some malarial backwater in West Africa. I remember France and Britain nearly went to war over possession of a mud fortress called Fashoda on the Upper Nile when I was eleven years old. You were just a baby then. It certainly seemed threatening enough at the time because I distinctly remember my father going into Enniskillen to ask about enlisting."

"Wasn't there a crisis in the Balkans three years ago?" asked Vivian, intrigued and impressed that his stepmother should recall such unfeminine matters so succinctly and so clearly. He listened attentively as she went on to explain the full extent of the crisis.

When she was finished, Dorothy fumbled in her bag for her silver cigarette case. Finding it at last, she lit two cigarettes, one for herself, the second for Vivian. In his father's absence, it hardly mattered whether he smoked the occasional cigarette or not, and she was well aware that he would have felt slighted not to have been offered one.

The pair puffed at their cigarettes in silence for a minute. Dorothy was inwardly amused by Vivian's determined effort to look like an habitual smoker as he struggled not to cough.

It was Vivian who spoke first. He enquired about the South African War, which she had mentioned. Dorothy launched once again into a rather expansive discourse.

Without either of them having been fully aware of it, Vivian's hand had been resting lightly on Dorothy's as she had been speaking. When suddenly she realized this, Dorothy felt a sudden warmth flow through her body and knew that she was blushing furiously in spite of the cool sea breeze on her face.

So he does want me, she thought with a thrill of excitement. He's mine whenever I want to lead him a step further. Not here, though. Not on the boat when there's so little time before we disembark in Calais. Dorothy laid her free hand on Vivian's, caressing his wrist lightly with her fingertips. Their eyes met for a long second before Dorothy, her resolution weakening, leaned forward and whispered, "I know how you feel about me, dearest. Believe me, I feel the same towards you, my sweet love, but we must both be very, very careful and very, very patient. There's much I have to tell you and even show you between here and Marseilles and perhaps now is, after all, as good a time as any."

Vivian's wondering eyes looked deeply into Dorothy's own before she recollected what she was about, hastily found a half-sovereign in the depths of her bag and pressed it into Vivian's palm.

"Vivian, give this to the steward. Tell him your stepmother is a little seasick and wishes to lie down for an hour in a quiet cabin without being disturbed. Do stress that, if you please, for an inquisitive steward or stewardess is the very last person we want disturbing us, my dear."

As Dorothy had surmised, it took Vivian no more than five minutes to arrange matters with a steward. She sighed with relief as Vivian shut the door behind them in a cabin no more than a few paces from that in which Clara and Iris dozed in one another's arms.

"Vivian, my love. How fine you look today. Come and kiss me this minute!" Their lips met as Dorothy impetuously pulled a willing Vivian onto the narrow bunk.

Vivian couldn't believe what was happening. How many nights had he lain awake in bed, naked, thinking about Dorothy? He had imagined this moment so many times, his hand easing his longing for her, picturing the flesh of his palm to be the wet flesh of her inner cunt. And now here he was kissing her. How sudden it all was.

He kissed her throat, her long slender throat upon which he had gazed so many times before. He had sat across from her at the dinner table and had watched her swallow and dreamt of laying his tender lips upon her neck. But she was so hurried, too hurried he thought, though certainly her quickness would be well-suited, if all turned out the way he would have it turn out, to the sudden throbbing ache in his penis. It was pounding against the tips of her trembling fingers that unbuttoned his white trousers and caressed his stiffening erection.

"Vivian, my darling. Time is of the essence so the silken dalliance about which we have both dreamed must be postponed until a later date. Do as I say and listen to what I have to tell you, for we may not have a second chance for a long time."

So saying, Dorothy pulled herself from Vivian's embrace and pulled off every stitch of her clothing, instructing Vivian to do the same.

Her body, though bent to fit into the bunk, was lovely. Truly he would like to see it in all its fullness, standing before him. He would like the chance, he thought, the luxury, to gaze upon her full white breasts, her slender long body, and to reach out to slowly to touch her. He would touch first her breasts as she stood before him, because for them he could not wait. Then he would touch her navel, her hips; he would run his fingers down the inwardly curving line of her hips until he reached the point where they once again flared out. Then he would reach behind and lay his fingers into the plump flesh of her buttocks, pulling her to him. Once she was close he would kiss the hair that covered her cunt. He would breathe her smell and thrust out his tongue to taste her humid flesh for the first time. But she was rushed.

A hurried search in her ubiquitous bag produced what she sought; an rubber condom obtained in London through the good agency of a hotel chambermaid's brother. It was one of several dozen now in Dorothy's possession.

Dorothy knelt and engulfed her stepson's erect penis in her mouth, much to his astonished delight. Her mouth was hot and through him rushed a wave of dizzying heat.

"Dorothy! Whatever are you doing?" Vivian gasped, knowing very well what his stepmother was doing as her determined tongue flickered around the dark red head of his firm erection.

Lifting her head to answer him, Dorothy replied with a smile. "Just getting you nicely wet so that I can slip this on you, sweetheart." She carefully unrolled the thin rubber of the condom onto his penis with her fingertips, patted the wrapped morsel with satisfaction and straddled him with consummate ease before carefully easing the slender shaft between the open petals of her cunt. She lowered herself down upon him until he was fully ensheathed within her.

Lady Dorothy Comerford sighed aloud with guiltless satisfaction and murmured, as though to herself alone, "How untarnished it rises from its bed of sweet curls. How modestly it bathes in my wetness. It is unobstructed within and straight without; it does not spread unrestrained and it does not branch out. It is good to behold from a distance yet tolerates every intimacy."

"Dorothy, my love, whatever are you saying?" panted Vivian, as astonished by Dorothy's words as he was enthralled by the measured sinuous movements of her hips and the sweet stimulation of her fingertips caressing his nipples.

"An improvised paraphrase of something Chou Tun-yi wrote about the lotus flower in eleventh-century China, my love. A silly whim of mine," Dorothy replied, leaning forward to kiss him lightly.

She kissed his brow and then his nose. She moved down to kiss his mouth. His lips were full and parted. He parted them even more to her insistent probing. She pushed her tongue into the space between his straight, white teeth and licked his tongue that had stretched forward to meet hers. She moved slowly up and down on his firm cock.

Dorothy's exquisitely-formed body rocked to and fro with increasing urgency until, shuddering, her climax caught her unawares and she collapsed atop Vivian, whose slender arms held her close and whose kisses soothed her perspiring face. His own urgency diminished as her thighs gripped him closely.

"Love is a visceral, not an intellectual process," whispered Vivian.

"No, my sweet boy, love engages the loins, the heart and the mind to be true and real. As our love is true and real, I mean. Now lie still and let me tell you what must be told before our second bout of love. Lie still and let your beautiful cock lie at ease, safe and warm in my little wet cunt."

"Now let me tell you what I've already told Clara and Iris."

As Vivian listened, breathless still from his rushed release, Dorothy proceeded to explain what had passed between herself and the two girls in the London hotel.

Dorothy's brief narration took barely ten minutes of uninterrupted time beginning with her account of her unwitting observation of the youthful trio at Dergvone, now so many miles behind them, and ending with an impassioned plea for the utmost discretion on the part of Vivian.

"You do realize, don't you, Vivian, that not so much as a flicker of suspicion can be permitted to enter the minds of your father, your uncle or your aunt. It goes without saying that the consequences of discovery are too horrendous to contemplate for an instant."

"Of course, Dorothy."

"And now, my sweet love, you might like to try fucking me from above. You see, the way we first made love, I controlled the pressure; this way you can control the pace and pressure."

So saying, Dorothy neatly detached herself from Vivian's grasp so that his half-erect penis slipped from her pink moistness with an audible "plop" which made them both giggle even as their bodies writhed awkwardly on the narrow bunk. Finally Vivian was above

Dorothy and her hand was squeezing and sliding up and down his responsive cock. When it stood stiff before him, Dorothy made sure that the rubber condom was in place. Then she guided him into her.

"Oooh, yes. That's it. Yes, Vivian. You're in me. Now push gently. That's it, in and out, in and out. Not too hard. Gently but firmly. Oooh, yes. Go on."

Vivian, determined to please his lovely stepmother, was every bit as careful and considerate as any of the few men whose love Dorothy had known in her young life.

As Vivian tentatively experimented, he began to discover that long strokes were what pleased him and Dorothy most. Alas, circumstances and his own youthful impatience precluded the leisurely, prolonged dalliance both would have preferred had time not been so pressing. Dorothy held him close, moaning softly and stroking his back with delicate strokes of her slender fingers. Suddenly, bucking her hips to meet his own thrusts, Dorothy squealed aloud in ecstatic release, heaving and tossing beneath him, her loins lifting instinctively to force him into her as deeply as possible. Her excitement triggered his own; his own passion met hers as his climax overwhelmed him and his back arched convulsively as he thrust into her before collapsing into her embrace.

"You see, sweet Vivian, how very, very, well we fit together, you and I."

"Mmmmm. Dorothy, darling, I never, ever dared to dream we'd be doing this."

"You know, Vivian, all things are possible if you really, truly want them."

"Everything?"

"Well, almost everything."

"Still, I can't love you *and* my two lovely cousins, can I?"

"Why not?" asked Dorothy archly as her moist brown eyes looked into his.

"You mean, it would be acceptable to you to share me with Clara and Iris?"

"Vivian, my love, we pass this way but once and love is to be seized when the opportunity presents itself. In a perfect world you and I could run away together and be happy ever after, but the world isn't like that at all. For one thing, I have almost no money of my own. For another, I have responsibilities to your father and the work he's doing for Ireland."

"Oh, Dorothy, if only things were easier!"

"Vivian, nobody ever told you it was easy being a grown-up, did they?"

"No. As a matter of fact, nobody ever did."

"Well then, you just have to grin and bear it. Life is less than perfect for most people most of the time and that's a fact of life that can't be changed at all. Now, keep very still, because I want to make sure that your little cowl hasn't come loose."

Vivian lifted himself and kept as still as possible while Dorothy's unseen hand fumbled beneath him. His flaccid penis was gently drawn forth from the moist, enfolding folds of her cunt.

"Good! The delights of motherhood are not to be mine for the immediate future at any rate. Which is, I need hardly add, a relief. The people who make these devices certainly know their business. Now, my darling, we must make haste and dress. Clara and Iris will be wondering where we are, that much is certain."

It was as Dorothy had foretold. Clara and Iris exchanged significant glances at the long-delayed reappearance of their cousin and his stepmother, telling Vivian in unmistakable terms that both had guessed the reason for the pair's prolonged absence.

It was Dorothy who spoke first.

"Remember what I told you girls about discretion. A little goes a very long way. In a very short time everything said and everything done will be under the watchful scrutiny of three other pairs of eyes so it would hardly be amiss for all of us to begin our enforced discretion here and now."

Clara groaned aloud, rolling her eyes upwards.

"You mean we can't talk about what you and Vivian were doing in that cabin alone together?"

"No, you most certainly may not and that's that! If you must know, I felt a little seasickness and Vivian was kind enough to procure a cabin and sit with me for a little while. That's all!"

Despite the mock-severity of her tone, Dorothy was grinning as she looked from Clara and Iris and then to Vivian, who looked away to hide his blushes.

A voice outside the window of their cabin could be heard informing a small boy that the French coast was no more than five miles away. It was with relief that Dorothy, glad to have impressed so vitally important a lesson on the two cousins, made her way up the metal-runged stairway behind Clara. Iris, her sketchpad under her arm, and Vivian, equipped with a brass-bound pocket telescope, followed closely behind her.

Unseen by her three companions, Iris experimentally touched her nipples through the thin material of her summer dress. Yes, she thought to herself in wonderment, her nipples were hard merely from thinking about what Vivian and Dorothy had presumably been doing together. She felt a sudden pang of irrational jealousy before remembering with a sigh of resignation that she was Dorothy's junior and that even her elder sister would certainly enjoy Vivian's embraces before she did.

It was at such times, Iris thought to herself with a quiet sigh, that life seemed so very unfair for a girl not quite yet a woman.

Still, France was getting nearer with every passing minute. Holding her sketchbook firmly as she leaned on the rail, she sketched a pair of gulls gliding by in the wind, and quickly sketched Clara clutching her straw bonnet and pointing out a fishing smack to Vivian and Dorothy as they stood beside her.

Dorothy's thoughts were of a more profound nature. Although dishonesty and dissimulation were not in her own nature, she knew that Clara and Iris were cautious enough to be carefully guarded in their speech and actions, for that was the way with sisters who spent most of their time in one another's company. It was Vivian who worried her most. Fresh from their amorous bout in the cabin below her feet, Vivian sparkled with an uncommon liveliness and vivacity Dorothy had seldom seen before. If this was to be apparent in his demeanor every time he spent an hour or two in sensual dalliance with Clara, Iris or herself, the transformation would be noticed and remarked upon. There was, Dorothy reflected, enough time to speak to Vivian about his new liveliness in the many hours that awaited them on the train to Marseilles.

She let a cigarette, her slender body hunched against the strong breeze, before laughing aloud with pleasure.

Whoever could have guessed that it would all happen so beautifully and so soon?

CHAPTER THE SEVENTH

FRANCE

VII.

The gleaming train raced through the countryside. Vivian thought carefully about the journey that lay ahead of them; the train in which they were travelling would take a little over twenty hours to complete the journey from London to Marseilles.

Dorothy's comprehensive travel guide to the Mediterranean's shores informed Vivian that the fastest train from Berlin to Odessa, the sparkling city on the Black Sea, took forty-one hours. How long then, he mused, would it take to reach Vladivostok by rail if and when the line was completed? Indeed, if it were feasible to span the shallow Bering Straits with a railway bridge sufficiently robust to withstand the pack ice of the winter months, the great Asian railway of the Russian Empire could be joined to the railway systems of North America and Mexico. It was a delightful thought—a railway system spanning the entire civilized globe. Already there was serious talk of a Berlin-to-Baghdad railway and even a Cairo-to-Cape Town railway, so why not a railway linking the vastness and riches of the Eurasian land mass to North America?

Vivian closed his eyes and began to visualize a complete railway network spanning the entire planet. The very pace of this long, splendid train was so very unlike the sedate dawdle of the modest locomotives which plied between Sligo, Boyle and Carrick-on-Shannon. How strange it should be, he thought, that minute Ireland should be so remarkably well-provided with railway lines reaching into virtually every tiny community on the remote, wind-swept Atlantic shore. The lines Vivian knew best connected Sligo with bustling Enniskillen, with the deep-water port of Galway, and with the soft, fertile lushness of the Midlands and Dublin to the east and with the great shipbuilding and manufacturing city of Belfast in the northeast. He thought dreamily of Dublin Bay; sparkling surf and white foam on the firm brown calves and exquisite buttocks of schoolgirls and shop-girls romping in the sunlit shallows on a half-holiday, their girlish voices loud with merriment and their eyes shining with glee.

A more intimate memory came unbidden to him; a summer's afternoon at Strandhill, less than a score of miles from Altavra and Dergvone. Strandhill, where the broad estuary of the Garavogue meets the island-strewn shore of the Atlantic, held memories of the very first time he had even really looked at his two lovely cousins. Clara, brimming with the enthusiasm of a novice, had helped him pursue a resplendent and quite rare butterfly over the dunes facing Coney Island, acrobatically wielding his smallest and lightest butterfly net. Undaunted by the brilliant insect's erratic flight, she had chased it even as it skimmed lightly over the waves to the safety of the sea-girt island. When she returned to dry land, empty-handed but convulsed with laughter, her saturated cotton dress had clung in almost classical folds to her delicious adolescent body, accentuating the ripeness of her firm, round breasts and her sun-dappled haunches.

When had that happened? he wondered. A moment's thought reminded him; it had been almost exactly a year ago. Iris even at that time had been given to smiling coyly at him whenever she felt herself free from her mother's prudent surveillance.

Lulled to somnolence by the rhythm of the iron wheels hurtling along the arrow-straight rails, Vivian fell into a contented slumber, his mind filled with thoughts of Clara and Iris.

Clara sat with closed eyes, but sleep was still far from her; her thoughts were of Donegal. She had not yet told Dorothy of her experiences in Belinda's studio-loft, although it would, she imagined with a secretive smile, be interesting to know what Dorothy would have to say on the subject. Clara rather wished that she had been equipped with condoms and diaphragms while a guest at Belinda's. What fun she and Belinda might have had with lovely young George then!

Perhaps even Belinda might have hesitated at the prospect of full consummation with George, although Clara doubted it. She licked her lips lasciviously, remembering the thrill of tasting George's copious offering of seed. The recollection made her wonder whether Vivian's would taste as exciting. Was it possible, though, that the actual taste was a quite separate thing altogether? Perhaps it had been merely the excitement of the moment that had made George taste so very delicious. It was all quite intriguing and puzzling, but now that Dorothy had begun to confide in the two sisters, answers would eventually be forthcoming to every question, no matter how odd or bizarre.

Clara stifled a reckless grin as she wondered what Dorothy's reaction would be on hearing Iris' curious tale about Elizabeth in Westport, for Clara was quite certain that Iris would sooner or later tell all to Dorothy. Possibly Dorothy had never even imagined that such depravity could exist, Clara thought as she turned her head to the window so that she might grin unobserved.

Clara glanced at Dorothy, who was intently poring over her guide of Northern Italy. Dorothy possessed everything a woman could possibly want, Clara thought with a fleeting pang of irrational and unfair envy. Even when Dorothy had been surrounded by conspicuously more chic and better-dressed women in the fashionable West End of London, her assured stroll was so graceful, her superiority so immediately evident, that heads invariably turned as she passed. Clara sighed, bitterly aware that in Dorothy's radiant presence she was completely eclipsed by the older woman and that she seemed no more than an awkward young girl from the limestone hills and green boreens of the West of Ireland.

Quietly, Dorothy pointed to Vivian and Iris who were fast asleep. "Just look at them, far, far away in dreamland," Dorothy whispered.

Iris was indeed, dreaming. A landscape of endless tree-lined avenues and swirling mists. A tall, majestically-turreted country house of dark stone in a mysterious landscape; marbled Ionic columns entwined in trailing strands of many-hued ivy; scores of ornate baroque urns of mossed stone, fantastically-carved balustrades fading softly into the mist as it advanced and receded.

Iris, her feet noiseless in this delectable landscape, walked boldly towards a tall gilded door, which opened unbidden before her. A sensation of enraptured delight filled her as she crossed the broad threshold. Inside, an enormous entry chamber was suffused with a deeply glowing incandescence. The walls were hung with rich tapestries of heraldic leopards, basilisks and gryphons. Sumptuously embroidered cushions the size of a slumbering grand piano were huddled in flocks in the midst of a kaleidoscopic sea of Oriental rugs whose fringes overlapped and interwove as though possessed with an inner life all their own.

Unsurprised, Iris gazed around her, her youthful face glowing with animation, her eyes shining expectantly; familiar faces surrounded her with seductive smiles. Carefully attentive hands disrobed her. She felt not the slightest apprehension or momentary misgiving as she was gently guided to a vast white bearskin luxuriously cascading over thick cushions. Iris felt herself gently lifted and as gently lowered. A hesitant protest rose within her only to die in her throat; was this not, she reasoned vaguely, what she most desired? Unseen hands eased her legs asunder, stroking her the while, caressing her whole body lightly and delicately. Iris felt herself weightless, as though free from the confines of her body even as every nerve of her being was responding to the insistent stimuli of her assailants' accomplished fingers.

Dimly perceived faces surrounded her—Elizabeth, Clara, Dorothy, Vivian and a half-score more...dimly remembered silhouettes and countenances of young men—and women—seen once or many times and instantly admired. She attempted to speak, yet was as one struck dumb. Iris shivered despite her elation as she became gradually aware of her audience and increasingly aware of that audience's mounting excitement. She, herself, was becoming more and more aroused. An image of a recurrent fantasy filled her mind: slowly undressing in front of a boy she liked and becoming increasingly aroused as she removed each successive garment.

Hands covered her eyes. A sleek, warmly feminine body loomed above hers. She felt another woman's firm nipples brush her own and a cascade of soft hair drape itself across her throat and face. A triangle of pubic curls touched hers, thrilling her despite her surprise. Was she, she wondered, repelled or enthralled? She was unsure, aware only of the tremulous excitement and arousal within her.

The vision of an anonymous woman making love to her before an audience swam in front of her unseeing eyes. She struggled against the hands that restrained her; the calm, gentle hands held her softly but firmly beneath the woman whose warm, sweetly-scented breath she could feel on her face.

A determined hand, oddly familiar to Iris, began to touch her splayed inner thighs with an insistent caressing motion, the knuckles barely brushing her outermost labia for what seemed an unendurably prolonged interlude. Suddenly a long, slim finger wriggled and writhed carefully into her pink moistness at the very same moment that the unseen woman's tongue entered her mouth and met the tip of her tongue.

An appreciative murmur ran through the invisible audience. Although tremendously aroused by the double stimulation of the careful finger and the agile tongue, Iris could hear subdued voices.

"Look at how lovely her young breasts are, how flat and smooth her little tummy is...."

"The delicate petals of her sweet cunt...."

"How utterly delicious she is. Just watch her beginning to respond...."

"Goodness, how delightfully sweet her cunt must taste. Like the purest honey...."

"Oooh, yes. Tasting her sweetness will be a delight...."

A ripple of exaltation coursed through Iris as the erect clitoris of the unseen woman touched her own. She cried aloud with the sudden pleasure of it.

"Iris!"

A voice, distinctively Clara's, was in her ear. Was Clara the woman loving her so skillfully, she wondered.

"Iris!"

The voice was louder and clearer this time. The tone of Clara's voice was pleasant, but not at all sensuous.

"Iris, darling. Please wake up!"

Iris' surroundings dissolved like a reflection in still water ruffled by a chill breeze. She opened her eyes to find herself in a railway carriage once more, the eyes of Dorothy, Vivian and Clara upon her.

It was Clara who spoke first.

"You were dreaming, Iris. It seemed such a pity to wake you, but you'd begun to murmur things."

Iris looked at Clara's knowing smile and blushed deeply.

"Things we were beginning to understand," added Vivian mischievously.

"It must be such an annoyance to be awakened from so beautiful a dream, but you were beginning to fidget and, well, touch yourself," said Dorothy in her kindest and most understanding tones. "The ticket inspector will be here within a minute or two."

Dorothy's eyes were half-closed, her voice a mere murmur.

Iris bit her lip, quietly bashful in the trio's presence now that she had rejoined the waking world.

She looked up shyly and her eyes met Vivian's steady gaze.

"Was I in your dream by any chance, Iris?" Vivian enjoined in a beguiling voice.

Iris nodded and blushed again, lowering her eyes.

"I think so. All three of you. It was a lovely, lovely, dream, too. What a pity it's over."

Dorothy spoke again, her voice relaxed and soft.

"Remember that dreams do sometimes come true, Iris. Perhaps we three can even make that particular dream, whatever it was, come true some day."

Dorothy yawned and willed herself fully awake.

"I must make sure that I have all our tickets ready because even First Class passengers must show their tickets when asked to do so."

A brief search within Dorothy's carryall unearthed the tickets for the ticket inspector, a sunburned man clad in an immaculately-tailored uniform and no older than Dorothy. His inspection of the tickets was brief, courteous and performed with nonchalant aplomb before he returned them, with the slightest of bows, to Dorothy. He was about to leave the compartment when his eyes settled on Iris, her face still flushed and warm from the arousal of her dream. He smiled softly at her, surreptitiously winking as he closed the door.

"Goodness me, Iris," breathed Dorothy, "you've certainly acquired an admirer in that young man. Now, Vivian dear, do stop looking annoyed. Jealousy and possessiveness are most unbecoming, you know."

Dorothy snapped shut her bag, replaced it on the seat beside her and closed her eyes.

CHAPTER THE EIGHTH

FRANCE

VIII.

Lyons was behind them now and Vivian could feel the warmth of the south upon his face on thrusting his head through the window briefly, his eyes averted from the locomotive's flying sparks and soot.

Behind him Dorothy dozed. Like Iris earlier, she was dreaming.

She lay fully clothed on a carved Jacobean four-poster bed in a room illuminated by silver midsummer moonlight streaming through an open window. Vivian and his two cousins knelt beside her on the broad expanse of lace; all three of them were, she discerned without evincing the slightest surprise, undressed already. Their moonlight-dappled arms moved with unhurried skill as they carefully unbuttoned her bodice and stroked her unfastened, flowing hair. Vivian's agile fingers removed her tight kid boots and tenderly fondled her stockinged calves and long thighs with leisurely grace. Equally adept, Clara and Iris uncovered her white breasts, murmuring subdued expressions of glee to each other for no more than a few seconds before their heads inclined and their soft lips and gentle white teeth began to caress her pink nipples, exciting them skillfully. Thirty fingertips touched her with lightly loving movements, fondled the hair that fell along the nape of her neck, scurried artlessly but gently beneath her black silk underskirt.

A thumb and its neighboring fingers parted her labia to allow access to the fingers of a different, smaller hand. Careful little fingers probed gently inside her cunt, tenderly touched her hidden, modestly hooded clitoris and lingered between the moist folds as though reluctant to leave her warm softness.

The most overwhelming emotions of sublime pleasure coursed through Dorothy. As though entranced, she was aware of the leisurely progress of the trio's amorous attentions. Vivian's subtle if still inexpert tongue lightly fluttered over the swelling organ Clara called a "butterfly," while Clara's own tongue met Dorothy's in a softly lingering kiss. She knew that the hands stroking and gently kneading her breasts were those of Iris, an Iris transformed from a blushing girl to a sexually aware young woman as adept in the arts of Venus as an accomplished young courtesan of Athens' golden age.

The petting continued without interruption, causing such irresistible pleasure in Dorothy's body that she no longer possessed the strength to resist the attentions being lavished upon her, even had she desired to.

"*Dux femina facti*," whispered Clara's sweet voice in her ear, mildly puzzling a joyous Dorothy quite lost in the throes of unimaginable rapturous delights. Vivian's untiring tongue flickered, darted, lapped and thrust into her, his actions calculated to excite, tease and caress by turn.

Quite suddenly, Dorothy squealed aloud with fulfillment and gratification, her cry echoed by the merry laughter of the trio into whose beaming smiles and amused eyes she found herself looking on opening her eyes. She gaped with somewhat embarrassed surprise; the excitement and the pleasure had all been no more than an exquisite fantasy just as Iris' dream had been.

"It appears that reveries of a certain nature are quite contagious on this particular train," chuckled Iris, playfully, if unconvincingly, attempting to sound disdainful even while her youthful eyes flowed with pleasure.

The remainder of the journey passed uneventfully. Not long after she had awakened, Dorothy dimly remembered a curious feature of her dream and turned to her stepson.

"Vivian, whatever does '*dux femina facti*' mean?"

Vivian thought for a moment, his brow furrowed as he stared through the window at passing pastures and forests, village spires and neat stone-built farmhouses.

"It could mean either that a woman began it, whatever 'it' might, be or—yes, this is a better translation—'a woman led the exploit.' It was something Clara found in one of her Latin schoolbooks only the other day. Why do you ask?"

"Oh, nothing at all, dear. Nothing at all."

Dorothy smiled secretively. Was there, she wondered, some strange telepathic bond growing between the four of them?

To Clara it seemed that the progress of the train from London to Marseilles had taken several lifetimes already, but the end was, she reflected happily, now in sight. They were due to arrive at

Marseilles within thirty minutes, assuming that they were on schedule.

Dorothy stretched herself languorously on being told of the party's imminent arrival at its destination.

"How easily it is for provincials like ourselves to be taken aback because other countries are so much bigger than our own tiny Ireland," she commented as Vivian and Iris bustled around the compartment organizing the party's varied and scattered possessions into orderly categories.

Clara nodded in agreement.

"France is so very, very big that I still have trouble comprehending it."

Vivian laughed with amusement.

"Perhaps it is as well that we are merely in France and not in the Russian Empire, dear Clara. The sheer immensity of Russia is too much for most Russians to comprehend adequately, let alone islanders like ourselves."

Clara and Iris stood by the window in the corridor, delighting in their first view of the great city of Marseilles. The train was perceptibly slowing amid clouds of steam and anguished screams from the unseen brakes beneath their feet.

At last Vivian had their possessions assembled to his satisfaction; the pile of personal baggage beside him at the carriage door was, he was all too well aware, was nothing compared to the collection of leather cases, stout trunks and hatboxes in the goods van.

"One might imagine we were leaving Ireland forever rather than for a few short weeks," he muttered aloud to Clara's amusement.

"Who knows, Vivian, we might even persuade your papa and mine to turn their abundant energies to improving French agriculture for a few years. Is an Irish baronet able to use his title here, I wonder? Would we have to call your papa 'Count Gerard Comerford?'"

"Surely that would be a little too Papal for an Anglo-Irishman, don't you think, Clara?" laughed Dorothy, who had joined Clara and Vivian as they stood beside the window in the corridor.

The train slowed still more. They clanked through the industrial suburbs of the vast and busy city.

Iris could barely restrain herself. Her parents, her uncle, and a totally new city awaited the four of them. What was more, Marseilles was merely the gateway to an entire new world: a world of new sights and new sounds, new tastes and unprecedented spectacles. It was all so very, very, thrilling. She was sure that a totally new existence was about to begin for her that very day.

As, indeed, it was, but scarcely in the manner Iris anticipated.

Dorothy felt a sudden chill of presentiment even while her young companions were gathered around her on the platform. Gerard was not, as she had expected, there to greet them. Neither James nor Prudence was anywhere in sight, either. Something, she knew instinctively, was amiss. Two men made their way towards the little party through the throng of travellers, their bearing and evident determination setting them apart at a glance. It was Dorothy who saw them first, anticipating Vivian's recognition by a heartbeat of time.

The taller of the pair, grave and subdued in an immaculate dark suit despite the searing Mediterranean warmth of the city, stepped forward and made a slight bow.

"Lady Dorothy Comerford?" he enquired hesitantly, with the merest trace of a Yorkshire accent discernible in his speech.

Without needing to be told that something quite dreadful had happened, Dorothy paled. She nodded wordlessly, her eyes beseeching the unknown stranger to continue.

The stranger, unnoticed as yet by Clara and Iris, motioned discreetly to Dorothy, wordlessly suggesting that she move some distance away down the platform in order to be certain that what he had to say was not overheard by the girls.

"Might I speak to you, my Lady…?"

Dorothy caught Vivian's eye. He had, she realized with relief, been aware of what was happening. A furtive movement of her hand brought him to her side. Sensing the urgency of the occasion, he had left what he was doing that instant and joined Dorothy and the two men. The man who had spoken introduced himself. He was, he explained, Mark Gurney, the British consul-general in Marseilles. He paused, cleared his throat awkwardly, and looked from Dorothy's face to Vivian's.

Ten yards from them, Clara and Iris stood silent and still, encircled by a parapet of luggage. Both sensed calamity.

"My Lady, I have to tell you that the most appalling accident has happened. Sir Gerard, his brother and his sister-in-law are all, alas, dead. It was very sudden, although that can scarcely be any consolation, I know. You see…."

Dorothy found the strength to interrupt him cooly.

"There is no possible doubt of this, is there, Mr. Gurney?"

"None whatever, madam. I was summoned to the scene myself by Francis Hamling, the junior vice-consul. He was in the main post office on consular business and was approached by a police officer who recognized him."

"When did this happen?"

"Early this morning. You see, your husband and the others were in a hired motor car with a local driver, a very experienced man as I've been informed, when a heavy goods cart careened down a slope and hit their car from the side, hurling it and its occupants into the harbor."

"So they were all drowned?" Dorothy's query was the merest murmur. Gerard, she remembered, had frequently dreamed that he was drowning in Lough Gara. Yet how far it was from Lough Gara to the harbor of Marseilles.

"When did you say this happened, Mr. Gurney?" enquired Vivian, calm and self-possessed in the face of such dire news.

"Shortly after nine this morning, sir," the consul replied.

To his own surprise, Vivian found himself taking immediate charge of the situation. He introduced himself to Mr. Gurney's silent companion, the deputy manager of the Regina Hotel, a man who immediately summoned a quartet of gleaming taxicabs to convey the party and their luggage to the hotel in which Gerard, James and Prudence had been staying.

To Vivian's great relief, Clara and Iris received the news with far more composure than he might have anticipated.

Dorothy sat in silence throughout the greater part of the journey to the Regina. Both she and Ireland had suffered a loss, she reflected. Of the two, Ireland's loss was surely the greater, for Gerard and James had both been men of a kind that impoverished and embittered little Ireland could least afford to lose. Complex and talented men, both of them, honest and altruistic landowners with independent and open minds, wide learning and a profound, if rarely articulated, sympathy with all that was most positive in contemporary Ireland.

Yet the immediate future had to be faced, a task for which Dorothy felt herself quite unprepared at that moment.

She turned to Vivian and spoke in a clear, even voice that surprised them both with its degree of self-possession.

"Vivian, dear, you are the heir to Gerard's title now, even if you may not be correctly addressed as 'Sir Vivian' until you are twenty-one. In the meantime, Clara and Iris are my wards under their father's last will. You weren't aware of this, of course, but both Gerard and James had parallel provisions in their respective wills to ensure that you, Clara and Iris were all duly safeguarded in the event of even the most remote eventuality. Vivian, you automatically become my ward now that Gerard is dead. Because James and Prudence died at the same time as Gerard, Clara and Iris are my wards, too. It means more responsibility in the long run. Naturally, it will take some time for me to become accustomed to the idea.

"Anyhow, one thing is quite certain. I shall be depending on you a great deal from now on. You can see that, can't you?"

Vivian said that she could rely on him absolutely. He had been thinking hard for the past quarter-hour. The dead were dead and could not be summoned back, however much one might desire it. So he and Dorothy, together with his lovely cousins, were at liberty to do as they pleased. In spite of the circumstances which had made such a state of affairs possible, Vivian was thrilled beyond measure at the prospect ahead.

Dorothy spoke again.

"I shall be needing your assistance from today onwards, in fact. Clara and Iris have no grandparents and their only close relative is an uncle, Prudence's older brother, who lives in New South Wales. One can hardly expect his intervention in any way. He did, after all, never come to regard the girls as his true nieces as they were not bound by blood ties. At any rate, I shall write to him today or tomorrow. His address, fortunately, is in one or other of my address books in my large valise.

"Vivian, I simply cannot bear the prospect of coping with the funeral arrangements and seeing to everything else that needs to be done. I really wonder whether..."

"Dorothy, please do allow me to take care of all that business. Mr. Gurney, the consul-general, will tell me everything that needs to be done and my command of French is no worse than yours. Perhaps we might consider burial locally; a city the size of Marseilles certainly possesses a sizeable British community, an Anglican church and a Protestant cemetery. There could be a memorial service at home in Ireland later on, you know."

"Vivian, are you telling me that there is no pressing reason for us to be in any great hurry to return to Ireland?"

"Exactly, Dorothy."

"I don't suppose there is, now that you put it that way. I can telegraph the bank at home whenever we need additional funds and the housekeepers at both Dergvone and Altavra are quite capable of keeping the two houses running."

Dorothy paused and looked through the window

of the taxi before turning to face Vivian once more. Her face was tear-streaked, her eyes moist. When at last she found her voice, its mellow huskiness possessed a note he had never heard before.

"Vivian."

"Yes, Dorothy."

"You won't leave me on my own tonight, will you?"

Vivian was taken aback for an instant, but recovered at once.

"I am completely at your service, Dorothy. Believe me."

Despite the incongruity of the grim occasion, they laughed softly together. Their fingers touched tentatively, unseen by either Clara or Iris. The two sisters, their tears wiped away, gazed intently at the busy city through the vehicle's windows.

The Regina, a hotel of the first class, was as sumptuously appointed as even Iris might have wished, mused Dorothy as she sat with the two sisters in their sunlit twin room looking out towards the cathedral and the sparkling sea beyond. At her insistence, the hotel's doctor had administered powerful sleeping draughts to both Clara and Iris and it was not until she was satisfied that both girls were fast asleep that Dorothy left their room and returned to her own.

Lighting a long-delayed cigarette, she permitted her thoughts to roam unhindered. She had married Gerard less for his title and his possessions than because she admired him for his ceaseless efforts to better a country in which men of his class were increasingly mere anachronisms. Undaunted, Gerard passionately believed it his duty to attend distant meetings of pig breeders rather than spend his leisure hours engaged in the more usual pursuits of his class. His articles, published in learned journals, popular magazines and illustrated monthly papers, dealt with rural self-sufficiency, rural roads, the economics of hard cheese production by small farmers, and much more of the same. Enough to fill a book, she thought with a wry smile.

Yes, that was it! She would see to it that Gerard's articles, notes and papers were published in a cheap edition well within the means of every farming household in Ireland. She clapped her hands together, pleased with her sudden inspiration. She would write to one of Gerard's more literary colleagues on the county agricultural committee and ask him to edit Gerard's posthumous papers, a task that would take several weeks, if not months of effort. Then she...

A discreet rap at the door interrupted her thoughts. She rose and opened it to reveal a combed, shining Vivian who entered readily and cheerfully at her gesture of invitation.

"I seem to have made a discovery, Dorothy. Our rooms have a connecting door. Here it is, behind this long tapestry. It was only by accident that I found the one in my own room."

Dorothy grinned as she realized what the discovery meant.

"So we can lock both doors leading out to the corridor and be together all night without the slightest apprehension of discovery or even suspicion, you clever, clever boy."

Vivian smiled and faced Dorothy before he spoke again.

"Dorothy, I do love you, you know. Well, I suppose I've loved you from the first time I saw you. What's more, I really love Clara and Iris, too. This is all, well, like a dream come true. Better than a dream, because it *is* true."

He strode towards her and seized her hands in his. When she looked up he could see a moistness in her wide eyes. Dorothy hesitated before she spoke.

"Yes, Vivian, I love you, too. It's a pity that we couldn't say it to each other before, but neither of us had any way of knowing this day would come, did we? We're here now, though, and that's what counts. Listen, Vivian, you make sure both doors to the corridor are securely locked and I'll run a bath for us both. Isn't it funny, having a bath right here in one's room? I wish we'd had one at Dergvone."

By the time Vivian had assured himself that both doors were securely locked, Dorothy had finished wrestling with the brass taps that poured water into the high iron bath standing majestically on its lion feet. Astonished at his own daring, he pulled her to him and kissed her. Their tongues met wetly and with a long-resisted longing.

Vivian's slim hands unfastened Dorothy's hair, freeing it to cascade down her back.

"No haste now, dearest. We have all night and an infinity of nights to come."

With great care, Vivian began to unbutton Dorothy's dress. The line of tiny buttons ran from the nape of her neck almost all the way down her back. He worked steadily, persistently sliding each button through its hole until Dorothy's green silk dress hung open. She leaned forward to assist him as he slid it from her shoulders, downwards over her breasts, sleek midriff and her gently curving thighs. She knelt to gather it neatly as it fell in shimmering folds at her feet.

Obligingly, Dorothy stepped daintily out of her dress and waited while Vivian folded it neatly and placed it on the end of the green velvet chaise longue, which stood beside the screen that almost encircled the bath.

"Well, you did that very well, Vivian. Perhaps you'd like to see how well you do when you take off my stockings."

Despite himself, despite his state of barely concealed excitement, Vivian felt oddly furtive and abashed as he slid his hands up Dorothy's legs and along her thighs until his hands reached the garters that held her soft silk stockings in place. At first he tried to ease both downwards at the same time, but he soon realized his mistake. So, transferring his right hand to join his left, he began to ease Dorothy's right stocking smoothly down until, at last, he was able to slide it from her foot.

Dorothy smiled down at him. She knew how impatient he was, but she felt that he'd remember and savor every detail of this first real night of love. It was something he'd enjoy recalling in later years, of that she was certain. Sexual pleasure, she mused, always required long preliminaries before the act itself. Haste and passion were all very well in their own way, but sexual love required more than a little finesse in order that one might derive maximum pleasure from life's greatest delight.

Vivian paused and looked up at her, his eyes sparkling with anticipation. Both of Dorothy's satin-smooth legs were bare now and she knew he awaited her next welcome command.

"You'll have to stand up to undress me completely, sweet Vivian. I'll show you how." Dorothy showed Vivian how to remove each undergarment with the very minimum of clumsiness and within a minute she stood naked before him.

Vivian's eyes swept over her lovely body. She seemed rather shorter than he had thought, now that she was barefoot. Whatever apprehension he felt was calmed when he looked at her gentle, willing smile. Then he allowed his eyes to descend to her perfectly symmetrical breasts tipped with small coral-red nipples, to her tiny navel and to the triangle of softly curling golden down at the juncture of her thighs.

"Well, Vivian, do say something. You mustn't be tongue-tied after you've undressed a lady, dearest. Our self-esteem needs a little flattery once we're undressed, you know."

"Oh, Dorothy, what can I say? You're...you're so beautiful, you really are."

"And what do you find so beautiful in particular, Vivian? Tell me what you see and how it pleases you."

"Well, your...your breasts are so full and smooth and lovely. I don't really know how to describe them, but they look so, well, so kissable and delicious."

"If they look so kissable perhaps you'd like to suit your actions to your words, sir."

At this, Vivian inclined his head and stooped to kiss Dorothy's nearer breast. As she felt his breath on her nipple, before his lips had so much as touched it, Dorothy could feel her composure slipping. His lips parted to allow him to take the small pinkness into his mouth and, as though he knew instinctively what to do, he sucked lightly and twirled his tongue speculatively around it. Dorothy became aware that both her nipples were hardening and that her cunt was becoming warmer and moister with every passing second.

Vivian put an arm around her, gently but insistently pulling her to him. His other hand found the breast hitherto untouched. His palm, roughened by his riding and fishing, rasped against the sensitive tissue, sending a shiver of delight through Dorothy. She fought with her own compelling desires and, to her surprise, won.

"That's very, very nice, Vivian. You certainly seem to know how a please a woman, don't you? Still, I'd like you to let go and undress yourself this very minute. We were about to take a bath together, remember?"

Reluctantly, Vivian disengaged himself and stood up to face her. Dorothy tilted her face, flushed with excitement she had great difficulty controlling, to kiss his lips.

"When you're undressed, my sweet love, you'll find me ready and waiting in the bath. Don't be too long, will you?"

Vivian undressed feverishly, hurling his clothes into a tangled pile. The tweed travelling suit, the soft white shirt with the amber cuff links, the shining black boots, the black wool tie and the white cotton underwear were all discarded within a minute.

It seemed ridiculous to Vivian that he should be embarrassed that his cock was in a state of semi-erection, but even so he wrapped a towel around his loins before taking the two or three paces to the corner of the screen and revealing himself to Dorothy.

To his relief, she didn't laugh at him at all. She grinned warmly at him and beckoned him to her, before reaching up and pulling at his loosely-secured towel. When it fell away she leaned to one side to cradle his slim member in her hand and inclined her head to kiss it. The silken ends of her hair landed upon it, dancing softly there before her moistened lips kissed the tip.

"Surprised you, did I, Vivian? Well, tonight is going to be quite a novel experience for you then, as well as being a very, very nice one, I hope. Come on, hop in. The water's lovely."

As Vivian eased his slim body into the warm water, it occurred to him that Dorothy was telling him what to do all the time. Perhaps the time, he thought, was ripe for him to take the initiative. With this thought uppermost in his mind, he lifted her foot to his lips and began kissing each toe in turn. Dorothy giggled and closed her eyes. If Vivian needed leading, she was ready and willing to lead him, but if he chose to take the initiative, she was equally happy, if not happier. Vivian kissed and caressed both of Dorothy's feet, stroking her insteps and ankles as he did so. Next, he ran his fingers lightly along her calves, using both hands to ease her legs apart.

Dorothy felt sure she knew what was to come next. She sighed deeply, her golden tresses cascading almost to the floor as her head arched back with delight when his fingertips brushed her open pussy's pouting lips. Once more she fought to control her instinctive response and won.

"Not yet, sweetheart. There's all the time in the world for that later. And a lot more besides. Just lie back and let me soothe all that urgency and impatience away."

Puzzled, Vivian lay back as best he could. The knobby brass taps were a few inches behind his head, yet he contrived to put his head between them and wriggled until he was as comfortable as circumstance permitted. Once he was still, Dorothy uncoiled herself and leaned forward.

"Vivian, darling, I'm going to play with this darling cock of yours. Then I'm going to suck and suck and suck until your seed spurts right into my mouth. Then I'm going to swallow every lovely white drop of it. Just lie still and relax. Don't be frightened, I won't bite your cock off; I'll be ever so careful and gentle, you'll see."

The effect of this short speech on Vivian's erection may be readily imagined. The penis Dorothy clasped was firm and stiff, its swollen head glistening with its immersion in the scented bathwater.

Dorothy knelt on the smooth enamel of the bath. She felt gratified that she had judged the desirable amount of water to within half an inch or less. Vivian's erection seemed almost to be floating as he lay back and sighed with pleasure. Dorothy, careless now of whether she wet her hair or not, squirmed forward and kissed the slim shaft before easing her fingers beneath it and bringing it to her lips. Her mouth encompassed the head, her tongue swirled around the tip, seeking and finding the tiny hole, causing Vivian to gasp aloud with unfeigned ecstasy.

Dorothy's right hand delicately manipulated the shaft, her thumb and the two determined fingers nearest to it manipulating the loose skin. Meanwhile, her left hand was busy, too. Vivian began to be aware of the complementary actions of the unseen hand, invisible beneath the water, when he felt a firm finger resolutely inserting itself in a place he'd never had invaded by a finger before. For a moment, he was tempted to protest, but surprisingly found himself enjoying the intrusion. Bit by bit, the finger was pushed through the tight ring of muscle. Then something unimaginable happened. Dorothy's wicked finger had found what it sought, known to Persian lovers as 'the almond inside,' and began to manipulate it with a light stroking action. Vivian found it so exciting, so blissfully stimulating, that with a convulsive thrust of his loins he spurted jet after frantic jet of what Dorothy had called his "seed" into the warm mouth that held the head of his penis in its velveteen embrace.

When Dorothy was certain that she had swallowed all there was to be swallowed, she carefully extracted the finger that had caused Vivian such thrilling and unexpected pleasure. She opened her mouth and, raising her head, smiled at him.

"I trust, my dear, that you feel a little less impelled by urgency now. One does not seek applause, of course, but it would be nice to know whether you found my attentions sufficiently up to your expectations."

"Dorothy, my love, my queen, what you just did was...well, it was delightful beyond words. I never knew that such pleasure even existed. How can I possible thank you or begin to repay you?"

"Easily enough done, my dear. First, let's get out of this bath and get dried, then I'll show you what to do next."

Vivian knelt and dried Dorothy with tenderness and care. He briskly toweled the few locks of her long hair which had trailed in the bath water as she had knelt to fellate him and, with even greater care, he patted dry the pink inner surfaces of her thighs and the deep cleft between her buttocks. Lovingly, he patted the damp curls on her plump hillock, leaning forward to kiss the soft hair again and again.

"Now, Vivian, I'm going to arrange myself comfortably and I'll leave it up to you to guess what would please me most. You must remember, though, that I'm in no hurry for your cock just yet. There's plenty of the night still ahead of us, so please don't be impatient, darling."

Dorothy sprawled on the bed, her legs overhanging its lower end. Her vaginal lips gaped wide open as, sighing with contentment, she spread her legs as wide apart as they would comfortably go.

Vivian guessed, rightly, that the appropriate posture for him to adopt would be that of a kneeling acolyte at such a temple of beauty. Accordingly, he spread a thick towel on the floor below the junction of Dorothy's legs and knelt on it, letting his eyes feast on the wealth of luxuriant curling hair and the coral-pink lips of her exquisitely lovely vagina.

His fingers lightly holding Dorothy's labia wide, Vivian inclined his head and kissed the rose-pink inner membrane softly. As he did so, he felt a shudder course through her. The visible excitement he aroused in her aroused him as well. His penis rose again before him. He wanted to touch it, but he knew it was Dorothy he must satisfy now, and truly he was dying to do just that. In order to make less insistent his own desire, he pressed his hardened penis to the bed against which he leaned. As he did so he imagined what it would be like to have his cock inside of Dorothy, inside this beautiful cunt that opened like a flower before him to admit his eyes and soon his fingers and tongue. He moistened his right index finger and inserted it carefully. There was no discernible impediment, so a second finger joined the first, as did a third moments later.

Dorothy sighed aloud. She had wanted a tongue rather than fingers, but she was content to let events take their course. Soon she would have Vivian trained to please in every way possible, a prospect which delighted her. As it would, indeed, delight Clara and Iris, too.

She shuddered with arousal as Vivian's left hand began to do to her what she had done to him in the bath so short a time before. A pleasing sensation, she mused, remembering the pleasure of Edward's unexpected and initially unwelcome attentions to that part of her.

Four fingers of Vivian's right hand were inside her and, to her immense pleasure, his thumb lightly brushed her clitoris. Without saying anything, she reached down and guided his thumb back to the conspicuous little ridge of engorged tissue. Vivian was such a fast learner, she thought with delight, as the fingers and thumb brought her, gasping and sighing, to her first orgasm with him.

"Vivian, darling, that's enough manipulation for now. I'm a sensitive girl and too much of that can make anyone quite sore much too quickly. Tell me, is your cock ready for action yet?"

"It is indeed. Anyway, even if it weren't, I'm sure you could make it as stiff as you liked in next to no time at all."

"Vivian, I want you to fuck me now. I want you to fuck me as fast and as hard as you possibly can." Dorothy's voice was weak in the wake of her receding orgasm, her breathing still labored slightly. This aroused Vivian even more, the sound of her weakened voice commanding him to fuck her hard. He scrambled to his feet, his cock thrusting out before him. Dorothy wriggled deftly up the bed, her long legs splayed, bending and stretching in the effort.

Vivian stood at the foot of the bed and watched her cunt as it closed and opened with her movements, as if it breathed in air she could not inhale by her nostrils alone. He watched her breasts moving from side to side, her nipples growing softer, fainter after her release. He wanted to have them in his mouth, to bring them back up to their full upstanding glory with his teeth and the dance of his tongue. He looked at her face, glowing with anticipation. She looked at him, and then at his cock.

"I want you, Vivian, to fuck me hard, to slam up into me hard and fast." She spoke slowly and deliberately. He felt as if he might explode right there, as if her words were somehow tangible, as if they were wrapping around his enraged cock. He had to be inside her.

He knelt on the bed and crawled toward her. When he was poised above her, his knees inside of her spread thighs, Dorothy took hold of his cock and placed the tip of it to the hot lips of her cunt. Both felt a rush of overwhelming desire when their flesh touched, his cock standing ready to open her lips further and drive in.

Then he arched his back, clenched his buttocks and thrust inside of her. She was wet, made more so by her fluids that had just been released, so the passage was easy. His cock slid in to its full length. He withdrew and thrust back in. He pounded in and out, one hand clutching her breast and squeezing it, the other hand propping him up so that all the while he could look down into her beautiful, seemingly agonized face.

"Harder, harder, fuck me harder," Dorothy very nearly screamed. Then she put her long legs around his back, wrapping them in a firm grip and pulling her buttocks up so that he could get inside her as deeply as possible.

"You can fuck and fuck and fuck me, yes, ah yes, yes, just like, just like, yes, like that, you can fuck me hard," moaned Dorothy. And when she could speak no longer because she could no longer think to speak, Vivian arched and thrust in so that the tip of his cock touched the innermost reaches of her cavern.

Dorothy pulled Vivian down onto her with her legs so that they were clamped together, panting and moaning. She could feel his orgasm coursing through his cock, pumping through the thick veins that ran along the underside of it, just as he could feel the walls of her cunt expanding and contracting and then slowly quieting.

It was not long before dawn that Dorothy yawned and reluctantly slid into slumber. Both doors were secured from the inside and she had given instructions that neither she, nor her charges, were to be disturbed before ten.

Vivian, exhausted, lay asleep beside her. A day before he had been a virgin. Now he was as sexually adept as many men twice his age. What she found as impressive as his eagerness and his stamina was his will to please. He had licked and tongued her several times; his foreplay, his prolonged pounding in and out of her and the exquisite bliss afforded by his triumphant climax were, mused Dorothy, as fully satisfying as any loveplay she had ever experienced.

As the Eastern sky began to lighten, Lady Dorothy Comerford fell asleep, her tousled hair lightly draping the sleeping form beside her.

CHAPTER THE NINTH

MADEIRA, JULY 1911

IX.

The month of July in that year of 1911 was pleasant and equable on the Atlantic island of Madeira. Over the eastward horizon the German Empire and the French Republic glared menacingly at each other on the scorched coast of Morocco. Further east still, Italy was poised to pioneer the use of the aeroplane as a weapon of war against the Turks and their Arab subjects in Tripolitania.

Vivian folded his newspaper with a long sigh. It was all too impossibly childish to be really happening, Vivian thought, yet each bellicose gesture, each loaded gun, each echoed threat, brought Europe closer to the impending catastrophe of a general war.

He glanced idly at the date on his newspaper. A mere five weeks had elapsed since the funeral service at the English church in the Rue de Bellois in Marseilles, yet so much had happened in those few short weeks. He smiled secretively, treasuring the delightful memory of his first true night of love with Dorothy in Marseilles and the many which had followed it.

Dorothy, his two cousins and he had stayed in Marseilles for a full ten days. As he had promised Dorothy he would, he had handled all the funeral and legal affairs, requiring of Dorothy only her signature on those documents which he, a minor under British law, was not permitted to sign. While all this was being left in Vivian's capable hands, Dorothy had spent her days, if not her nights, with Clara and Iris.

Little by little the two girls, with the resilience of youth, had recovered from the shock of the sudden loss of both parents. During their enforced sojourn in Marseilles, Dorothy and the girls had been made welcome by the sizeable and prosperous British community of that great port.

One vivacious and voluble young woman had become particularly close to Dorothy and her charges. They had spent many hours and days in her company, becoming frequent luncheon and dinner guests at her lovely home on the Chemin d'Endoume, and had been delighted to accept her invitation to a stay of some weeks at her family's residence on Madeira.

Barbara Arouca was hardly a year older than Dorothy. Her aristocratic Anglo-Irish lineage was as immediately discernible in her ineffable self-confidence and proud bearing as in her aquiline nose, determined jaw and lithe, slim figure.

As the wife of an immensely wealthy Anglo-Brazilian trader, she was accustomed to travelling from one to another of the Arouca family's residences, following her own whims and caprices as readily as her husband's commercial and social commitments.

In the course of a luncheon party at her tall house overlooking the old port and the ancient crenellated defenses of Marseilles, she had remarked, en passant, that she would soon be travelling to Madeira to escape the tedium of an entire summer spent in the city. With barely a pause for breath she had then invited Dorothy and the three young people to be her guests at her house overlooking Funchal, the principal town of Madeira. Her description of the island had excited and delighted Clara and Iris, whose gleeful response had immediately persuaded Dorothy to accept Madame Arouca's invitation without further discussion.

Clara and Iris had enjoyed the voyage from Marseilles to Madeira immensely, delighted by the flying fish and leaping dolphins of the glittering Mediterranean. En route they had eaten heartily and had eagerly attempted to communicate with their fellow-travellers in the smattering of phrase-book Portuguese they struggled to memorize each day.

Now, reclining on the balcony of the Arouca villa, basking in the warmth of the generous sun, Vivian closed his eyes, picturing Barbara Arouca's slim form as her husband and, no doubt, her lovers, saw it. With a tingle of self-reproach he banished the lingering mental picture of Dorothy's full breasts and sleek thighs to concentrate on his vision of Barbara's radiant loveliness. Her hair, dark as liquid graphite, cascaded onto exquisitely-formed white shoulders; her long, narrow back curved inward dramatically at the waist before swelling out subtly to define her delicately-shaped hips and the delicious expanse of her buttocks and pale thighs.

Erotic excitement stirred in Vivian as the image of Barbara grew sharper in his mind. He imagined the sensation of nuzzling her lush breasts with a despairing sigh.

It was a pity, he mused, that Dorothy was not available at that very moment, for he found himself craving the fulfillment and release her insistent caresses would bring. Instead, he glanced around the terrace to see who was in sight. He unbuttoned his white linen trousers upon seeing no one and took his erect penis out.

He thought of Barbara, how she would look undressed before him, as he wrapped his fingers around his penis, which now sprang free of his trousers. He glanced around again, checking to see that no one was in sight. His cock was warm and hard in his hand. The hot sun beat down on the tip of it and spread like hot liquid down the shaft, increasing the pleasure that was igniting his body. He thought of Barbara climbing onto his supine form, her white thighs straddling his own, her cunt wrapping around his cock. His hand worked up and down, pumping and squeezing as he closed his eyes. It was not long before his fluid spurted out of him onto his belly. It was hot, as if heated by the sun, and seemed to land like points of fire on his flesh.

Afterwards, he fell asleep in the sun. When he awoke, he began thinking of Barbara again. And again he became aroused. It irritated him, just then, that he should be yet again aroused, that his penis should harden at the mere thought of the woman. He rose to go inside. His desire was not, thankfully, as persistent as it had been earlier. He went upstairs.

At the threshold of his bedroom he paused on encountering Rosa, the young housemaid whose parents and grandparents were house servants of the Aroucas in Rio. Smiling broadly and not in the least deferentially, Rosa turned to look at Vivian as she was about to leave the room. Uneasily aware of his aroused condition, Vivian glanced down to see for himself if his hard penis could be discerned beneath his trousers. Rosa's amber-hued eyes followed his glance. With an enchantingly lewd grin, she cast aside the feather duster her hand had been gripping up to that moment, darted past a dumbstruck Vivian to turn the key in the lock and, spinning round, threw her dark satin arms around him.

Vivian was so taken aback by this sudden onslaught that he was still gathering his wits when he felt her sharp white teeth biting the lobe of his ear. A determined small hand deftly unbuttoned his trousers.

A discreet murmur in accented Portuguese, "Oo, jjame v-lo," which Vivian later translated to his satisfaction as "Oh, let me see it," was the crowning touch. Whatever his loyalties to Dorothy might be, Vivian was all too well aware of the effect on his senses of the agile hand now burrowing in his underpants.

With a little yelp of glee, Rosa found what she sought. Her other hand was rapidly unfastening the waistband of his trousers so that in less time than it would have taken Vivian to describe, Rosa had half-pulled, half-pushed Vivian's garments down his thighs and was excitedly stroking him, holding his slim tool as securely as might a tropical tendril grasp the stem of a young tree. Her warm lips met his and her little pink tongue flickered in his mouth, exciting him quite unbearably. Rosa was certainly a most exciting young girl, thought Vivian, and a very graceful young girl, too. She was no older than Iris, of that he was sure, yet the determination with which she pushed him backwards onto the silk cover of the carved mahogany bed was hardly the action of a timid virgin.

Almost before he had kicked his trousers from around his ankles, he felt himself straddled by Rosa's muscular young thighs. Her sweet voice, as musical as that of an exotic bird, tinkled in his ear, "*Calma, menino, eu farei tudo.*" Vivian knew this was a demand that he lie still and let Rosa take charge.

An accomplished hand held him as if in a grip of steel as Rosa, with a combined giggle and sigh, lowered herself onto his lance. Her calf-length skirt rode up to her waist, revealing a delectable triangular copse of blue-black curls overshadowing the deep crimson softness of her cleft. The sensations she was inflicting on Vivian were by now such that it seemed he was almost on the threshold of pain. Unseen rippling muscles were gripping and relaxing, relaxing and gripping in a way that dear Dorothy had probably never so much as dreamed was possible.

Maybe Dorothy would like Rosa to instruct her in the technique, he thought with a flash of inner amusement. He laughed aloud and, reaching out, clasped Rosa to him with one lithe arm. The giggling girl squealed with glee as he held her close and used his free hand to seek and find the ridge which every girl and woman possesses. Vivian gasped with surprise as he realized that Rosa's clitoris was—and there could be no doubt about it—both larger and firmer than Dorothy's. Rosa writhed with the delight of unashamed sensuality under Vivian's careful caresses, stretching her slim arms over her head when he lifted her dress and removed it. He immediately began worrying her wine-dark nipples with attentive teeth.

Rosa was whispering in his ear again. Vivian strained to catch what she said so that he might mentally translate every word mentally as soon as it was uttered. To his surprise and pleasure, Vivian understood her demand that he thrust harder.

"*Agora, empuza...um pouco mais forte.*" The girl murmured incessantly as she bounced up and down on his rod.

Vivian felt his climax coming, but something held him back despite his own urgent passion. What he really wanted, he realized with the sudden itch of inspiration, was to have this lovely creature's sweet mouth receive his copious libation.

It took a little while for Rosa to comprehend what he wanted before she sprang up with an exclamation of delight and rearranged herself. She spread her thighs to either side of his head and lowered herself so that she could lean down to take him into her mouth and have his tongue rise up into her. Her soft warm mouth readily engulfed his stiffness, while her agile pink tongue slid wetly around its ruby head.

For his own part, Vivian played his tongue flickeringly across Rosa's bright crimson butterfly, while he buried his eager nose in the neat triangle of dark curls and sniffed her natural fragrance luxuriously.

A sudden thought occurred to Vivian: how intoxicatingly exotic Rosa, sweet, charcoal-shadowed Rosa, both smelled and tasted compared to Dorothy's now-familiar odor and flavor. He found himself wondering vaguely whether Clara and Iris, sisters if not by blood, but by upbringing, tasted similar. It would be good, he thought, to have them both together someday in the near future. His fingers stroked Rosa's angular hips. His nose nuzzled deeper into her warmly enfolding petals as he nibbled and tongued her engorged clitoris anew.

A bird sang outside the window as, without warning, Rosa, the soft wetness of her mouth still firmly clamped around Vivian's erection, bucked wildly and wove her slim buttocks and sharp hips rapidly from one side to the other in a fit of ecstasy.

Her climax precipitated Vivian's own; he arched his hips thrice, dreamily aware of Rosa's restrained, ladylike swallowing as she avidly drank every drop of his pearl-pale essence, tasting each swallow with mounting pleasure, still sucking fiercely until there was, at last, no more to be had.

Her soft voice, when at last she raised her head and spoke, seemed to Vivian to be coming from a great distance, "*Foi delicioso, rapazinho*," which Vivian quickly guessed meant, "That was delicious, you lovely boy."

They lay together like contented kittens in a basket. Vivian let a gentle exploratory finger stroke Rosa's high cheekbones lightly, while the palm of his other hand lightly rubbed the area just above her pronounced tailbone. She purred with gratification. He licked the warm, dewy dampness of her silky skin, pleased to hear her sigh aloud to be so caressed.

Rosa's slim brown legs, dappled in the afternoon's warm sunlight pouring through the tall windows curtained with delicately patterned Madeiran lace, stretched with feline grace. Vivian ran his fingers pensively through her soft mane and leaned over to kiss her nose lightly. Responding languidly, Rosa reached out until her fingers playfully tickled a limp part of Vivian which duly rewarded her ministrations by stirring slightly as if girding itself for a renewed bout of love.

Vivian wriggled from her grasp, pulled Rosa abruptly to him and kissed her ardently.

Breathless Rosa responded, "*Voc um rapaz lindo*," which Vivian took to be a declaration that Rosa considered him to be a lovely boy. To hear the sweetly alliterative vowels of this subtle tongue delivered in Rosa's honey like voice was, he felt, blissful beyond words. With Rosa's help he could be speaking Portuguese of a limited kind in a matter of days, he thought.

It was a still, hot afternoon. The morning breeze had died and every sound carried unhindered for miles in the unmoving, heavy air. Vivian vaguely recalled Barbara's explanation that this heavy dullness never lasted long on the breezy heights of the Monte, certainly never longer than an hour or two, while it often lasted for the greater part of the day at Funchal, the main port of the island.

Vivian, drifting into slumber, snuggled close to Rosa despite the heat of the day. The distant clatter and whirr of the rack-and-pinion railway linking the Monte with the port alerted Rosa. With the grace of a startled deer she jumped to her feet, wide-eyed, before kissing Vivian wetly and urgently. She wriggled into her maid's costume as rapidly as she had discarded it earlier, watched by a lazily satiated Vivian.

He would, he knew, have been ready enough for a repetition of Rosa's ardent and delicious attentions, but guessed that she knew, by habit as well as by unfailing instinct, that Barbara Arouca, Dorothy and his two cousins were almost certainly aboard the toylike train. He yawned. There was no urgent necessity for him to be present when the troupe of four women entered the house. Rosa had vanished from the room so that she might be conspicuously industrious when the mistress of the house and her entourage appeared. Vivian yawned again, stretched and fell into a dreamless slumber, unaware that the door of his room was unlocked.

No more than ten minutes had elapsed before a discreet tap could be heard at Vivian's bedroom door. Vivian, however, dozed on. The tap was repeated and still met with no response. The door handle turned softly, the door was opened from without, and Clara entered the room on silent feet. Perceptive Clara took in the scene at a glance. Vivian lay naked on the bed. On the floor beside the bed lay a feather duster. Clara's sharp eyes observed something another observer might have missed, a tiny jet-black curl of hair on the snowy silk of the bed. Curious, Clara licked the tip of her finger, applied the moistened fingertip to the curl and brought it close to her eye. It was, she was certain, one of Rosa's hairs. The same housemaid whose feather duster lay on the floor at Clara's feet.

"Incriminating evidence indeed!" muttered Clara to herself before examining the curl more closely. There could be no doubt that this particular curl came from Rosa, nor could there be the slightest doubt as to which part of Rosa had shed it.

"So, sweet cousin Vivian, our dear Dorothy is insufficient for your needs, is she?" murmured Clara before turning to lock the door behind her. She returned to the bed on which Vivian slept and knelt on the red-patterned Turkish carpet at its side.

This incongruous *mise-en-scène* amused Clara mightily. She had sought Vivian to inform him that the evening meal was to be a candlelit lobster repast on the terrace. There had been no thought of erotic dalliance in her mind, yet Clara was scarcely one to turn down an opportunity for intimacy such as this!

"And now, my dear cousin, let us see whether you can please little Clara's palate as well as a certain young boy in Donegal once did," said Clara softly before taking Vivian's limp penis between her warm palms and inclining her head.

"Lucky little Rosa, to have taken the sweetness

from this darling sugar stick," whispered Clara. She extended her tongue and tentatively licked the extremity of Vivian's dormant organ.

"Mmmmm. Every bit as sweet as the taste of dear George. What's more, dear Vivian," she addressed her cousin, still lost in the enfolding arms of Morpheus, "there's rather more of you in Clara's virgin hands than young George had to offer and my not-so-innocent mouth will wake you up in a moment or two, of that you can be certain." So saying, Clara popped Vivian's cock into her mouth and closed her eyes. With disarmingly casual ease, she let her tongue flick hither and thither as her mouth slid up and down Vivian's limp shaft. It was with only a momentary twinge of disappointment that she realized Vivian's member tasted so impeccably clean that only one explanation was possible. So the maid had sucked her dear cousin dry, had she? Remorselessly applying the brief experience she had garnered in Donegal, Clara used both hands to assist the meticulously careful ministrations of her mouth. She giggled inwardly as a thought occurred to her; if Rosa had tasted Vivian's every drop, had he tasted her feminine nectar? The very thought thrilled Clara's fecund imagination. Surely if Vivian's tongue could please an amorous young wench like Rosa, her own tongue could do the job far better.

Clara shuddered with delectable excitement at the memory of the first time she had parted Iris' pale thighs and hesitantly extended her tongue into the moist cleft beneath her sister's russet triangle of curls. Iris, she remembered, had exhibited excitement and timidity at one and the very same time, a pleasingly salty bouquet had met Clara's tongue and risen sweetly to her nostrils as her lips and pink tongue-tip had met the bright salmon-pink of her warm, sweet younger sister's inner warmth and sweetness.

The prospect of tasting Rosa's hidden delights sent a ripple of excitement through Clara. Should she attempt it alone or share the girl with Iris? Or would it be more interesting to share her with Vivian? The vision of the possible combinations and intriguing activities thrilled her. How would Vivian like to be lovingly fellated by two girls at once? By his cousin and the maidservant acting in unselfish harmony? Would he relish the prospect of watching the two young women amusing themselves before him to refresh his ardor?

Even while Clara was musing thus, she was aware that the morsel in her untiring mouth was responding in a most gratifying manner to her attentions. The head of Vivian's member was swelling so much that it tickled her tonsils to thrust her mouth too far forward; the shaft was growing perceptibly fatter and rounder with every passing moment.

Vivian stirred and mumbled something. He was, realized Clara, in that twilight between slumber and wakefulness some people recognize as being the soul's most vulnerable time. Reluctantly, Clara lifted her head to look at Vivian's beloved countenance. For the briefest of moments a stalactite of clear saliva, caught between her lower lip and the tip of his radiant shaft, shone in the afternoon sunlight.

"It's me, sweet Vivian. Clara. Your Clara has you in her loving hand. Don't be nervous, darling."

Clara sprawled beside Vivian and awakened him with wetly ardent kisses. Her right hand ruffled his hair, her left stroked that part of him on which her attentions had been so laboriously bestowed.

"Clara? You?"

He was still only barely awake, thought Clara. She kissed his ear and whispered, "Yes, darling. Me. You will let Clara have what you let that darling little maid enjoy, won't you?"

There was a note of almost wistful eagerness in Clara's dulcet tones. As Vivian struggled into full consciousness he lay still, responding to his lovely cousin's sweetly affectionate kisses with kisses of his own while his mind raced.

So lovely Clara was eager to blow him, was she? Vivian could well remember the many times he had fantasized about just such an eventuality. Indeed, had the circumstance been as he had so often pictured it, he would have readily begged her to take him in her mouth. Yet here she was beseeching him to lie back and let her savor what giggling young Rosa had so recently tasted.

The improbable irony nearly caused Vivian to shriek aloud with mirth, but an inner voice restrained him. If that was, indeed, what Clara wanted to do, she was welcome to do it. But…here he thought hard…it would be all the more memorable an occasion if he were to make her beg to do what he would have eagerly begged her to do himself. When he spoke his voice sounded oddly imperious even to himself.

"Clara! Whatever do you mean?"

"We must regard each moment as an eternity with neither present nor past and take the goodness it offers without fear."

"Clara?"

"It is only thus that mortals may participate in the felicity of the gods, the bright gods who feed on happiness forever."

"Clara, I'll let you suck me until I shoot my sperm into the furthest reaches of your darling throat, if that's what you want. Is it?"

"Oh, Vivian, you know that's exactly what I want. You are ever such a dear, you really are!"

There are a few conditions you have to meet first, though, my lovely Clara."

Clara looked at her cousin, her eyes sparkling with excitement. This was more and more like a fairy story. If Vivian wanted preliminaries, he could have them all. The very thought thrilled her. "Vivian, tell me what they are."

"Well, first of all, I'd like you to see if you can take both my balls in your mouth at once."

"Both of them? Surely that isn't possible, Vivian. I'll certainly try, though." Clara was about to dart her head to the scrotal sac below her cousin's erection, still firm in her warm hand, when Vivian grasped her by the hair and pulled her back to him with an abrupt jerk.

"That isn't all, slave! After you've done that to my complete satisfaction, I want you to lick my bottom. Really lick it, too. All along the crack and inside!"

"Vivian?"

"It's quite clean, Clara. I had a bath not five hours ago, after my swim." Vivian sensed that this admission sounded like weakness on his part, so he hastily added, "Then you're to let me give you a really good spanking until I decide you've had enough."

"Whatever for, you beast?" demanded Clara, annoyed that Vivian should have the temerity to think of such things as a condition for his permitting her to do something she was quite certain he would greatly enjoy.

"As your punishment for all the times you and Iris excited me so unbearably at Dergvone, knowing full well that I had to slink away and finish the job by hand when either of you wicked girls could have done it for me in a moment."

"Were we really so cruel?" asked Clara, visibly softening.

"Yes, you jolly well were. What's more, you knew it, too."

"Well, sir. Is that all, or is there yet more?"

"That's all for now, slave. Begin with my balls and use that little mouth of yours as gently as if you were carrying eggs."

Sensing that Vivian wanted her to display as much servility as she was capable of mustering, Clara put her hands together in a submissive gesture and wriggled and squirmed until her face was on the same level as Vivian's balls.

All through the exchange she had kept Vivian's cock enclosed in her hand. Now she relinquished her grip sufficiently to run her sinuous tongue up and down its length to tantalize Vivian before bending her head to engulf his matching pair of plums in her eager mouth.

The task was far easier than she had imagined. First she sucked one into her mouth, then the other. Her tongue rolled around them, caressing the enclosing sac with an avid relentlessness that surprised her. Her nose nuzzled and butted the underside of Vivian's swollen shaft as she let her fingers gently brush along its length. If Vivian wanted her to play the role of a slave girl, well and good, she thought. The day would surely come when the tables were turned and she, in her turn, would demand equal satisfaction and more. In enforced silence, she pondered what adequate retribution might be appropriate for Vivian even while her lips and tongue labored to satisfy his wishes.

Perhaps it would be possible to compel Vivian to satisfy Iris, Rosa and herself with his lips and tongue until he pleaded exhaustion. Now that would be a fine spectacle, would it not? Clara glowed with inner satisfaction at the very thought.

Like her own present labors, it would be less of an ordeal than a rite of passage which Vivian would remember with pride forever. Clara's contented reverie was interrupted by a sudden cry from Vivian.

"Clara, please stop! Please!"

Clara raised her head. She noted the appeal in Vivian's voice and was interested to know what effect her attention had had on him. As though reluctantly, she pulled her mouth from Vivian's now glistening sac and spoke softly.

"Master?" Clara's voice had all the sweetness of amber and the softness of silk.

"Oh, Clara! That was lovely. Unbearably good, really it was." There was a note of arousal in Vivian's voice that was new and interesting to Clara.

"Does my master want more of the same, or does he want the second task to begin now?"

"The second task?" Vivian, in his excitement, had quite forgotten.

"Master's bottom is to be licked and nuzzled by his humble slave. If my master would be so obliging as to roll over perhaps the licking could begin."

Having said this, Clara deftly altered her position until she was able to roll Vivian's limp body over so that he lay face downwards on the broad bed. She parted his legs and eased his buttocks asunder.

"Lie still, now. Your slave is about to do your bidding as best she can until she is ordered to stop."

By this time Clara's feelings were in a state of turmoil. What had begun as an almost distasteful imposition was turning out be a quite delightful series of exciting novelties, she thought as her tongue lightly stroked the furrow between her cousin's firm buttocks.

A low moan from Vivian reassured Clara.

How simple it seemed it was to please men if this sort of thing was all that was required, reflected Clara as her tongue darted into Vivian's tight anal aperture and he sighed aloud once more. Caressing Vivian was less easy now than it had been when she had sucked his scrotum and its contents, but she discovered quickly enough that she might easily stroke and fondle the backs of his thighs, his buttocks, his back and his scrotal sac as her tongue tickled his secret passage. There was no unpleasant taste, no distasteful odor discernible as she teased him, provoking a tiny movement in that most sensitive of places as though a tiny mouth were returning her kisses with long-repressed affection.

Then she reached her hand under him. Vivian lifted his lower body in order to accommodate the passage of her hand. Once under him, she grabbed hold of his stiff cock and squeezed while he pushed into her grip as if she were beneath him and he were pushing deep into her cunt. He pushed and pushed against her hand while she continued to lick the space between his buttocks.

"No more! Please, Clara. I simply can't bear any more. Please stop."

"So the slave has passed the first two of her tests, has she?"

"Oh, Clara. How can you ask? I love you to distraction, my sweet, sweet cousin."

"Do you, indeed, Vivian? I wonder whether you truly do, for love is a folly of the mind, an unquenchable fire, a hunger without surfeit, a sweet delight, a pleasing madness, a labor without repose and a repose without labor. Is that what you really mean?"

"Goodness, Clara, that's exactly what I mean.

Every word of it. Whoever put it quite so neatly and so well?"

"A thirteenth-century poet called Richard de Fournival. I'm glad I memorized it because it just about sums it all up rather neatly, don't you think? It certainly sums up the way Iris and Dorothy and I all feel about you, Vivian."

"Really? All of you?"

"Well, Iris and I certainly do. Dorothy has doubtless told you herself how much she loves you. Still, we haven't finished yet, have we?"

"Finished, Clara?"

Clara stood up and laughed softly, her hands on her hips. With an abrupt gesture she spun on her heel, brought an upholstered leather dressing-table stool to the bedside and, raising her skirt and underskirt to her waist, bent over it most uncomfortably. Her toes and her fingertips brushed the carpeted floor as she stretched to her fullest extent.

"Do you really want me to spank you, Clara?"

Clara nodded. Even if Vivian's spanking was vigorous, she felt sure that the excitement she would derive from it would be thrilling beyond belief.

"Clara, my sweet love, I simply couldn't spank you after what you've done to please me today. Really I couldn't."

"Vivian, you are a little too forgetful, you know. I shan't suck your cock until I've been well-spanked first. I mean it, too."

"You mean a hard spanking, don't you?"

"I do. This time I shall add some conditions, too. I want twenty smacks on each buttock, delivered alternately. After every five smacks you are to pause and lick my bottom just as I licked yours. When you've done everything to my satisfaction, I shall squat on your face while you tongue me as thoroughly as you tongued that saucy young maid earlier.

"Then, and only then, will your Clara give you the sucking she's been longing to give you for weeks without number. Do you understand, Vivian?"

Vivian nodded speechlessly.

"Good. You may begin to spank me now."

With that she bent over the table. The first contact of flesh, his hand to her buttocks, was startling, but too soft. Clara reprimanded him, saying "Harder!" and then "Harder still!" Only then did Vivian relinquish his fear of hurting his dear cousin and begin to spank her hard, his hand stinging and leaving behind its blazing print on her tender flesh.

After five spanks, he bent his head and licked her bottom, his tongue sliding along the entire line of the convergence of the two halves and finding its place in the tight round hole. Clara hadn't felt this kind of excitement before. Her cunt ached. It was a dull, throbbing ache in comparison to the stinging of her buttocks and the coolness of his tongue.

Vivian resumed the spanking, his hand coming down hard and loud on her flesh. Clara winced visibly each time his hand came down. Vivian, who continued mercilessly, didn't know what was worse, the prints left behind on her flesh by his hand, or the cracking sound it made. When he had delivered nearly all the blows he had been commanded to give, he bent down to administer his cool tongue, which to Clara was like a salve to the enflamed burning of her flesh. He licked her tight hole that gaped open. His cheek felt the heat of her buttocks as it rested against them while he licked around the ridges of her contracting orifice. He imagined what it would be like to stick his thick cock into such a small hole.

Clara was in agony. Her buttocks stung terribly

and her cunt ached from having not been touched and from its close proximity to his obedient, eager tongue. Vivian then slid his tongue down from her bottomhole. Instead of drawing it away from contact with her skin, he continued, sliding it down until he had to kneel on the floor to be able to reach where he wanted to go.

Clara felt his tongue sliding down and under her. Then she felt rush through her the sweet recognition of his tongue on the wet open folds and inner flesh of her cunt. He probed inside and licked her hidden clitoris. How full of power and strength his tongue felt to her, as if it possessed all the force of an army, so many tiny explosions did it send through her body. And yet, he hadn't finished the job. She demanded that he continue with the spanking, and that were he not to finish, she couldn't fellate him.

Vivian stood up once again and resumed his spanking. This time Clara took her finger to her cunt. She touched her clitoris and rubbed it back and forth. She rubbed it while feeling acutely the stinging blows landing on her behind. Just as Vivian was bearing down with the last blow, Clara began to come. She yelled, "Harder!" and Vivian's hand came down harshly, stinging hard and hot on her buttocks, enflaming her tender, red flesh. Her bottomcheeks clenched even tighter to brace themselves against the onslaught of both Vivian's furious hand and her furious exploding orgasm.

Afterwards she pushed him back on the bed and licked at his penis as if her tongue were a growing fire. She licked rapidly and sucked hard until he came, releasing his fluid in a thick, warm stream down her throat.

CHAPTER THE TENTH

MADEIRA

X.

Barbara raised her glass of cool Portuguese wine in a gesture of salutation to her guests. A bat fluttered in pursuit of an erratic moth between the palms below the terrace on which Dorothy, Clara, Iris and Vivian sat spellbound by the eloquence of their hostess. The evening was flower-scented and voluptuously warm.

"I promised you girls an interesting surprise while we were in Funchal today and, since I always keep my promise it shall be revealed in but a moment."

Vivian sipped his wine and looked quizzically from one face to another, only to be met by four amused, secretive smiles. No clues were apparent on any face.

"Alas, dear Vivian, you were detained here at Villa Arouca and unable to visit our charmingly provincial little capital. Still, I am given to understand that my staff endeavored to make your stay quite comfortable."

Barbara smiled in Vivian's direction before continuing in a softer tone, "The remarkable plant of which I was speaking earlier is, curiously enough, commemorated in one of the place names of Marseilles. You see, the Cannebire—which, as you know, runs from the old harbor to the Cours St. Louis—used to be a rope-walk of the same kind as is to be found in many ports and dockyard towns. Few citizens of Marseilles would associate the name with the hemp plant, of course."

"What is the connection, Barbara?" enquired Iris.

"The Linnaean name for the hemp plant is 'cannabis,' my dear Iris. The plant was known to the herbalists and healers of classical antiquity for its miraculous powers. Indeed, it was probably known to the people of Europe, Africa and Asia long before the first city was ever built or the first written symbol painstakingly inscribed in wet mud.

"In Brazil, just as in Morocco and the other parts of North Africa, it is widely used as an intoxicant with quite engaging qualities."

"Surely you don't mean people eat the plant used to make rope!" Clara demanded, her eyes wide with interest.

"Well, it can be eaten; indeed, it is sometimes used in cookery. More usually, it is smoked or crushed into a sweetened drink. In some countries the essence is compressed into a sort of greenish-brown cake known as kif or hashish."

Dorothy's eyes had grown wide as Barbara had been speaking. She glanced around furtively before whispering, as surreptitiously as one might murmur an aside in a crowded social gathering, "Do you have just a little for us to try, Barbara?"

Barbara's laugh was merry and light.

"Of course I do, Dorothy. The father of the man who supplies our milk grows a few square meters for me somewhere in the hills. It was such a bore to have it sent from Brazil at dreadfully irregular intervals, especially since communications with my dear friend in Tangier are so unreliable with this silly crisis going on between the unspeakable French and those interfering Germans."

Barbara Arouca raised her hand in a beckoning gesture and a manservant approached as if on cue, bearing a cigarette-box on a silver tray. Bowing slightly, he left as silently as he had come.

"All the house servants here are to be trusted absolutely," observed Barbara softly. "Not only Rosa," and here Barbara paused as if to take a deep breath while she winked at Vivian, "but all of them. Jacob's father and grandfather were both in the service of my husband's family in Brazil, just as were Rosa's grandparents and possibly even her great-grandparents."

She leaned towards Clara conspiratorially and added in a stage whisper, "My dear, when you have a household of your own, as you will someday, be certain to select your servants primarily for their discretion. Everything else is quite, quite secondary. A discreet servant can be taught competence, but an indiscreet servant, no matter how thoroughly efficient he or she may be, can seldom be taught discretion so easily."

Clara looked at the pattern of writhing dragons on the lid of the little box and enquired airily, "Barbara, are you telling us that this hashish is illegal here in Madeira?"

"Actually what we have for our delectation tonight is not hashish, Clara. For that you will have to wait until you visit my dear, depraved friend in Tangier. The cigarettes in this box have been hand-rolled with the most potent leaves of the cannabis plant itself."

"Goodness, Barbara, how very, very thrilling and delightfully wicked," interjected Dorothy, while

Vivian and Iris, who had followed every word of the conversation most intently, stared entranced at the patterned box glittering in the candlelight.

"Is it actually unlawful here in Madeira?" asked Iris, echoing Clara's unanswered question.

"It is not actually illegal, my dear, although doubtless it will eventually be deemed a danger to public order and prohibited. Nonetheless, it would be distinctly unwise to mention the subject in inappropriate company or to saunter about in public while obviously under its influence."

"What is the actual influence, Barbara?" Vivian asked, unsuccessfully attempting to conceal his impatience.

"Vivian, enough procrastination is enough. Allow me to light one for each of you." Barbara opened the box by depressing a concealed button which made the lid spring open. She extracted five meticulously hand-rolled cigarettes, one for each of the party, and lit them carefully one by one before passing them down the table.

"Draw the smoke well into your lungs and hold it there for as long as you can without having to fight for breath. Release the smoke slowly through your nose. Refresh your palate with a sip or two of wine, then repeat the process as many times as you can until the cigarette has been entirely consumed."

Dorothy and Vivian, Clara and Iris, did as Barbara told them. The silence was broken only by a subdued cough from Iris.

At length Vivian looked around the party and asked, "Is that it? Is that all there is?"

Barbara laughed lightly. "How very like a man! Impatience always! Impatience and haste in everything. My dear Vivian, wait for a few minutes and sip your wine. Magic spells are never quite instantaneous, you know. Look at your watch and make a note of the time. Perhaps you'd care to tell me after twenty minutes or so have elapsed that the divine herb has had no effect on your system."

Barbara rang for coffee and Grand Marnier.

There was a long silence at the table. Barbara poured the coffee and the Grand Marnier while the fluttering bats, attracted by the moths circling the flickering candles swooped and soared inches above everyone's heads.

"It is curious how one is apt to be scared of bats in one's childhood," observed Clara with the air of a philosopher uttering a profound truth.

"It is irrational to be apprehensive of bats," answered Dorothy. "They are, after all, no more than the German name states them to be, '*die Fledermaus.*'"

"'Flying mouse,'" giggled Iris.

The girls began to laugh aloud, helplessly. Dorothy laughed until the tears ran down her cheeks. The whole world, bats included, was beautiful beyond description.

"Recite 'An Ode to A Bat,'" demanded Dorothy of nobody in particular. Clara, Iris and Vivian were in the grip of helpless mirth, so Dorothy began an ode unaided.

"O, creature of the lambent,
purple haze-filled twilight,
As orange sunset turns rip-
ples of lavender sea into
luminescent goldfish scales,
We love your grace,
your…your….

"Oh, do help me out someone; I simply have too many pictures in my mind and far too few words."

Her voice trailed away helplessly before she began to giggle as uncontrollably as Clara and Iris. A cool voice intruded.

"Vivian, tell me something, if you please." It was Barbara who spoke.

Vivian smiled at Barbara, a radiantly beautiful Barbara framed in the glowing candlelight.

"Yes, O Goddess Divine, keeper of the sacred bats. What can I do for you?"

"Tell me, have twenty minutes passed since I asked you to look at your watch?"

"My watch? When did I look at it last?"

"When I asked you to do so, a mere fifteen minutes ago."

All eyes of were on Barbara.

"Now do you think the sacred herb of two hemispheres has had no effect upon you, my dear Vivian? O, bronzed and carefree boy with your beguiling eyes and wanton pleasures, tell me now what you feel."

"Incredibly carefree and happy," replied Vivian.

"Do you all feel the same way?" enquired Barbara of Dorothy, Clara and Iris. All nodded in response to her question.

"Have you ever had sensations like this before, pictures and images in your minds like this? Have you ever felt so truly loving and loved?"

A silence greeted this last enquiry, a silence broken by Clara's puzzled question: "So this is why governments and priests disapprove of it?"

"Exactly, my dear. So long as the divine herb is restricted to the poorest of the poor and to a handful of the prosperous decadent like myself, there is no call to take measures against it. As soon as it becomes available to the great mass of the people, it is perceived as a threat to the harmonious order of society."

"What society calls 'morals' is simply blind obedience to command," said Iris softly.

"Exactly, Iris," replied Barbara with a tinkling laugh.

"You understand many more things than one might expect of a girl your age, my dear. Perhaps you would care to tell us about Plato's ideal city-state before the magic of the sacred herb wears off. As a subject it offers more scope than that of bats."

With eloquence and passion, Iris proceeded to build up the bright walls and sparkling palaces of the city within her. She related everything she knew on the subject, her knowledge, it seemed to her, proliferating as she went on.

When Iris was finished, Barbara clapped her hands and added brightly, changing the subject, "Tomorrow, we shall all take a long excursion in the interior of the island. We shall ride on wonderfully wiry and sure-footed Andalusian horses and drink Malmsey, the wine in which Shakespeare saw fit to have a king drowned, on the slopes of the Areeiro."

"So now to bed, for surely we must start early," sang Dorothy.

"And we shall, I trust, smoke a little more of this truly wondrous herb?" queried Clara, who had been absorbed in the spectacle of a gecko pair engaged in vigorous courtship on the balustrade.

For no particular reason that he could think of, Vivian paused in the hallway of the villa en route to bed. Still quite lightheaded from the remarkable cigarette and in no hurry to retire for the night, he strolled into the salon. What he saw astonished him.

The great houses of the relatively few wealthy families at home in Ireland were impressive enough, with their small armies of servants, their packs of hounds and the endless rounds of lavish entertaining.

A tiny handful of the really wealthy were able to afford the plurality of houses, the steam yachts, the villas in the South of France, the stables filled with thoroughbred horses and even, though it was never mentioned aloud in the presence of the young, discreet establishments in Dublin and Kingstown for pretty young ladies.

Yet this house, which was merely the Aroucas' Madeira residence, was completely unlike anything Vivian had seen in Ireland. The floors were a kaleidoscopic, almost living, assemblage of Oriental carpets and rugs of differing hues and textures. Some were bright enough to be dazzlingly garish, others were subtle and more subdued. A few were severely geometrical, their patterning emphasized and enhanced by the meticulous hand-clipping Vivian knew was called embossing.

The furniture was every bit as imposing as the carpet-strewn floor. A seventeenth-century Chinese cabinet on a gilded stand stood between a carved sandalwood door and a matching pair of tables faced with countless facets of mother-of-pearl. An Elizabethan cupboard of dark oak, carved in ornate writing scrolls, appeared to hover above a Chinoiserie cabinet glittering with many-hued dragons and swirling clouds.

Vivian turned slowly to savor the salon's contents at his leisure. Above a marble mantelpiece, decorated with carved garlands of fruit and flowers, and a classical mask representing Diana, goddess of the moon and the hunt, and brace of patient caryatides flanking the jambs, was a portrait of their absent host, Philippe Arouca. The portrait was in a style vaguely familiar to Vivian. Philippe Arouca, a long-limbed man whose face reflected his maternal Gallic ancestry, sat on a heap of neatly-piled bales and sacks. On each sack and bale was the name of the commodity it contained, stencilled in Portuguese and French. Rubber, sugar and coffee predominated, noted Vivian, as he translated the words under his breath. Through Arouca's hands trickled gold nuggets and precious stones while the background of the painting was a detailed portrayal of what was evidently a sugar plantation.

The effect, somewhat astonishing at first sight, was pleasing. Evidently Philippe Arouca had no hesitations about proclaiming himself to be a man made wealthy by dealings in the raw materials of his native Brazil.

"Aha, sweet Vivian, there you are!"

Dorothy and Barbara joined him in the salon, glasses of Grand Marnier in hand.

"Vivian, Barbara and I were talking on the terrace after you vanished. Without consulting you, we girls—all four of us, that is, including Clara and Iris—decided that rather than a mere day's journey to the interior, it would be far more agreeable if we were to take a longer tour and take Rosa with us as a maid-of-all-work. I do so hope you agree."

Dorothy beamed with delight as Vivian readily expressed his assent.

Languidly, Barbara added, "It will give you an opportunity to visit parts of the island few foreigners ever have a chance to see. We shall swim from tiny beaches on the North Coast, feast beneath the stars and, perhaps, indulge other appetites besides. The expedition will, I trust, be a fitting climax to your stay on Madeira."

Vivian, noting Barbara's tone, enquired softly, "Are we to assume that you are, perhaps, leaving Madeira so soon yourself, Barbara?"

Barbara Arouca inclined her head with, Vivian thought, more than a little sadness.

"Alas, yes. I received a telegram from Philippe

today. He is about to sail from Rio to Europe and it seems that he desires my presence in Antwerp and Amsterdam.

"Oh, I shall enjoy the social round well enough once I am in Northern Europe once more, but I do so love this house, the groves of trees, the warmth, the friendliness of the people and, above all, being mistress of my own household. Still, let us not dwell on such things; we shall explore Madeira like triumphant conquistadors, disport ourselves like Dionysians and indulge ourselves like Epicureans of old. What's more, I shall give you letters of introduction, duly preceded by telegraph, to my wicked friend Anna Laudanska in Tangier, who will show and tell you much that is entertaining. I shall also give you letters of introduction to some truly wonderful Japanese friends of mine in Gibraltar."

Barbara turned and left the room, leaving Dorothy and Vivian alone together. Dorothy drew her stepson close and affectionately nuzzled her ear.

"Look, Vivian, Barbara gave me two of those wondrous cigarettes for the two of us to smoke together upstairs. She guessed at once, of course, that you and I are sleeping together. Indeed, she went so far as to congratulate me on my good fortune in being surrounded by such beautiful young people. Not that you should become conceited because of that chance remark, of course, my bronzed and lovely boy!

"Goodness, look at the time! Let us go to bed and see whether Barbara spoke truly when she whispered to me that this herb of hers possesses aphrodisiac qualities for which it is famed throughout the world."

Following Barbara's example, Vivian and

Dorothy sped upstairs. From the bedroom shared by Clara and Iris came the sounds of rustling and giggling, distinctly audible through the panelled doors as Vivian and Dorothy hurried along the corridor. Dorothy laughed softly.

"Vivian, I do believe those cousins of your have found the slim volumes Barbara put in their room earlier this evening. Deliciously naughty little books, they are. You shall see them for yourself soon enough, dear heart. Perhaps it would be interesting for you to peruse them in the company of Clara first. As the elder of the two, she is entitled to take precedence over her sister.

"Goodness, Vivian, I do believe you are actually blushing! How very unlike you."

Once Dorothy's bedroom door was softly closed behind them, they lit the first hand-rolled cigarette from one of the tall candles flanking the bed.

Vivian steadied Dorothy's hand, took the glass of liqueur and sipped from it. Together they smoked the slim reed, patiently alternating it between them until it was exhausted.

Vivian's mouth leaned close to Dorothy's ear and his warm breath sent shivers of delight through her. He nibbled her earlobe, then suckled it. His gentle fingertips traced patterns on Dorothy's neck and throat that excited feelings of the most exquisite pleasure.

"Go on, Vivian. Please go on. It's as though you're playing beautiful music on my whole body."

Vivian caressed the silky texture of her hair, cupped her cheeks with his rough palms before tracing the contours of her shoulders and arms. Dorothy's eyes were closed; her whole body was beginning to surrender to the rhythmic surges of the erotic sensations within her. Vivian's warm mouth was in the hollow of her throat, pausing before following the path between her breasts.

"My goodness, Vivian, how very, very skilled you've become since we first made love." Vivian didn't lift his head to reply; his tongue was describing a shrinking circle around her right breast until he felt the texture of her skin change as he reached the areola. Dorothy gasped with pleasure as he drew the nipple into his mouth and Vivian felt a flush of heat throbbing in his loins as his fingers matched his tongue's movements on her other breast. His suckling was gentle at first, but as Dorothy urged her body against his mouth he found himself increasing the pressure. Dorothy breathed hard and caressed his head. She adored lengthy preliminaries, Vivian knew, and tonight seemed special somehow. Perhaps it was the magical effect of the herb they had all smoked, perhaps it was the half-remembered promise in Barbara Arouca's cryptic reference to "other appetites" they would enjoy in the days to come.

As though in a trance, he applied himself once more to the task of pleasing Dorothy. His mouth sought hers and their lips met. His soft lips worked downward and found her throat again and drew wet spirals around her other breast until he reached the awaiting nipple. Dorothy pushed herself up to him, shuddering with delight as his mouth responded with a sharp tug.

"Oh, Vivian, you do it so well, my love. My sweet, sweet love. Go on, I beg of you."

Vivian's careful fingers caressed her flat stomach, her rounded hip, her long thighs. Slowly, he reached for her inner thigh, feeling Dorothy's firm muscles ripple as she tensed before relaxing to part her legs. In a moment his fingers were cupped over her hillock of golden curls, sensing the warmth in the cleft below.

He whispered in her ear, "Dorothy, my sweet, you are so beautiful, like a goddess in a myth, like Venus herself."

"Goodness, Vivian, what imagery! Like Zeus, are you going to transform yourself into a swan, a shower of gold, or a bull before you fuck me?"

As Vivian's tongue touched Dorothy's moist labia, he looked up at her, illuminated in the candlelight. Dorothy purred with joy, her back arched and tensed with anticipation. Unhurried, he buried his nose in her soft triangle of sweetly-scented pussy hair, kissed her ardently and lowered his head. Dorothy's whole frame quivered with pleasurable anticipation of what they both knew would come next. Vivian's long fingers spread open her folds and his exploratory tongue sipped her nectar with an epicure's unhurried ease.

"Oh, Vivian, I can feel your tongue exploring every ridge and fold. This is the most marvellous night of love we've ever had and you aren't even inside me yet, are you?"

As though in response, Vivian shook his head violently from side to side, letting his nose buffet the inflamed ridge Dorothy had taken to calling her "butterfly between the petals" ever since she had spent a languid hour or two in conversation with Clara and Iris.

"Oooh, Vivian, if Clara and Iris ever learn you can do that, I'll never have you all to myself again. Goodness, it's driving me crazy. Do it some more right now."

Vivian's remorseless tongue teased Dorothy's small, erect center of delight. In reply, she squealed aloud, heedless of who might hear her in the stillness of the night.

"Fingers, Vivian. Put...put your fingers in...in

me! Right up inside my cunt!" Dorothy wriggled and sobbed with ecstasy as, with two fingers, he probed gently into her moist passage and pushed tentatively upwards from the inside. Dorothy's back arched convulsively and she cried aloud again.

Distantly, Vivian could hear girlish giggles and briefly wondered whether Dorothy had heard them as well amid her excitement.

Dorothy, however, had not. Her hands clenched and relaxed spasmodically in an unconscious beckoning motion that matched her convulsive breaths.

"In me, dearest. Come into me now. I want your stiff cock, your lovely prick inside me."

Experienced as he now was, it took Vivian mere seconds to reach for, and fit, a condom from the bedside table. Then, as Dorothy arched her hips and spread her flowerlike cunt to receive him, he slid effortlessly into her moist, warm depths.

"So now I'm in you, my love, my queen. Is that what you wanted?" he teased.

"Oh, Vivian. If only you knew how good your prick feels in me! Let me hold you close."

Vivian drew back and thrust hard into her, delighting in her cry of pleasure. Dorothy's long legs wrapped themselves octopus-like around him to draw him yet more deeply into her, savoring the exquisite feeling of her throbbing cunt caressing his full length.

They made love with reckless abandon, Dorothy's throaty cries and hoarse yelps ringing through the room and, he guessed, the rest of the house. He rammed his cock into her, drawing back until his cockhead was just inside the folds of her pussy, then driving in fully until his balls slapped her upturned buttocks.

At last the tension approached its peak; both

could feel it gathering in their loins as Vivian drew his hips back, his fingertips caressing the tight aperture between Dorothy's curving buttocks, an activity which always gave her the profoundest pleasure.

Relentlessly he thrust hard into her again and again as, sweating and moaning, she clung to him. For what seemed like an age, a paroxysm of release surged through him as Dorothy thrust herself to him with every nerve and sinew taut and screamed his name aloud.

They lay together, panting from their exertions. Dorothy, her voice a breathless sob, crooned, "My darling love, that was the best yet. The best ever in my whole life, I swear it. Vivian, did I make noise? I'm a little bit ashamed if I did, but who cares?"

"Well, sweet Dorothy, you were just a bit noisier than usual, yes."

"What an advertisement for your prowess, Vivian! They must all have heard me, you know. Barbara's room is opposite ours, so she must have heard me, not to mention your young cousins longing for you to slide your prick into their moist little slits. There's the housemaid, too. Rosa. She must have heard us. I've seen the way she looks at you, you know. Barbara was telling me that Rosa has some interesting accomplishments. The sort of accomplishments that would interest you, I'm sure."

"What sort of accomplishments do you mean, Dorothy my darling?"

"For the answer to that question you'll just have to wait and see."

"You mean Barbara told you that Rosa is going to display these remarkable accomplishments of hers on our expedition to the interior of Madeira? In front of all of us?"

"I rather think that Rosa's displays require one or more participants from the audience, Vivian. Barbara didn't go into detail quite as much as I would have liked, but I'm sure all will be revealed in due course. Barbara rather likes surprises, as you've probably gathered."

"So we just wait patiently until Barbara decides that the time is ripe for her maid-of-all-work to reveal her secrets?"

"Yes, but I don't think Barbara will keep us guessing too long. I rather think tomorrow night might be interesting, you know."

"Well then, we must wait until tomorrow night, I suppose."

"Vivian, I am not prepared to wait until tomorrow night for another fuck. Come, let me suck your cock to its full size again and then you can have me on my hands and knees like a rutting animal. I know how you enjoy to have me like that!"

Vivian kneeled before Dorothy, who sat up to take his penis, which was hardening instantly at the mere mention of having her on her hands and knees, into her mouth. She sucked on him until his cock was adequately hard and then let him slip from the hold of her lips. She kissed the tip of his cock and tongued the small hole before getting onto her hands and knees. Then she told him to drive into her hard. He braced himself at her hips and placed his cock between her legs after sliding it down the line of her buttocks. Then he pushed into her, immediately finding the hole that he sought. He looked at her back, her spine struggling, it seemed, to cut through the blanket of her flesh. Some of her hair lay spread on her back and some of it fell to the side of her face. He knew that her breasts hung pendulant and untouched so that the rather large points of her nipples just reached the surface of the bed. With his hands on her hips he pulled her back onto the length of his cock and then pushed her away so that just the tip of it remained enclosed in her folds.

Then Dorothy began her own movement. She sat back onto him and circled her buttocks slowly so that he could feel his cock circling inside of her. Then she leaned forward again and pushed back hard. He couldn't bear it. He pulled her and pushed her and she helped him, the muscles in her legs working as hard as the muscles in his arms. The wetness in her cunt made the pulling out and pushing in easy and exquisite for Vivian. Soon he was thrusting deeply into her and moaning as she was sitting back heavily onto him. She took her finger to her clitoris when she felt him starting to come, and manipulated it roughly so that she came at once.

CHAPTER THE ELEVENTH

MADEIRA, AUGUST 1911

XI.

"Clara, listen. There's something very strange about the herb, the cannabis, in the cigarettes we smoked last night."

"Gracious, don't I know it, Iris. Did you mean something special, though?"

"Well, yes, I did. For one thing, I felt very peaceful and omniscient, very old and wise after I felt the effects. Endlessly old, possessed of a memory going back forever in time. A memory coming out of the Middle Ages and far, far beyond that, even. I felt like the primitive savage from whom we are all descended; a believer in devil-worship and the power of the stars, dancing beneath the new moon, naked and tattooed and holy."

"You mean like a cave dweller?" queried Clara as they rode side by side along the rock uphill path.

"A cave dweller and a dweller on the islands; a contemporary of mastodons, mammoths and saber-toothed tigers; full of the lusts and terrors of the great pre-glacial forests."

"Go on, Iris," urged Clara, her eyes wide with interest.

"Older even than that, Clara. I felt like an arboreal ape with all its instincts. In fact, I really had to make an effort, a very big effort, not to pounce on Vivian and pull all his clothes off right there on the terrace."

Clara laughed prettily as the wind ruffled her hair.

"So you felt as though you had great claws and eyes that see in the dark and a long prehensile tail? It's just as well you didn't tell me, otherwise I would have been quite nervous about sleeping in the same house, let alone cuddling up in the very same bed."

Both laughed aloud, startling a green lizard clinging to a rough stone wall bordering the uphill track leading to the interior. Their journey, Clara reflected, had started while the birds were still laboring over the first tentative notes of the dawn chorus. By now, with noon approaching, the day would have been unbearably hot had it not been for the gentle but persistent breeze coming, as Vivian had painstakingly explained after consulting his travel guide, from the distant African coast.

"How strange it is to see the gorse and heather again," said Iris, admiringly.

"Almost an Irish landscape so long as one doesn't look too closely," replied Clara, her gaze taking in the evergreen underwood clothing the slopes. Speaking in an undertone so as not to be overheard by the others a few yards ahead, she added, "Wasn't it exciting hearing Dorothy squealing and roaring with delight while Vivian was fucking her?"

"Goodness, yes. I only wish he'd be a little more attentive to us, though. Do you realize that Vivian has hardly even kissed me for weeks now?"

"Listen, Iris, I know Vivian's still interested in you. After all, he can't think you're too young any more, because..."

Awkwardly aware that she had begun to say something ill-considered, Clara flushed and turned her head away. Iris, however, was not to be deferred so easily.

"Clara, dear sister, I rather think you are keeping a secret from me, you know."

Clara shook her head, biting her lower lip furiously.

"Now, Clara, let me think hard and I'll try to guess what it is, shall I? You said that Vivian cannot think me too young, didn't you? Now why would you say such a thing, I wonder? The only reason that makes sense is that you caught Vivian in the embrace of someone my age, or maybe even younger. Well, well, Clara, how very exciting that must have been for you!

"I wonder what your reaction was? Were you humiliated and mortified that Vivian preferred the embraces of a younger girl to yours, or were you equal to the situation? Did you pull the little trollop's legs apart and let your tongue flick in her moistened cunny, I wonder?

"Perhaps you taught her all the things you've learned while you've been practicing your arts on me, sweet sister of mine!"

Iris regarded her older sister with an ironic smile before continuing her teasing. "One has to try to guess the identity of this engaging young maid. Was it the local slattern who brings the milk perhaps? Or the niece of the English couple staying at the Monte Palace Hotel, the plump girl with the dark brown eyes?

"Yes, Clara, I think I can picture the scene now. The girl came to pay a social visit only to find Vivian alone in the house. Within minutes he had her pinned down, she wailing piteously that she is a good girl, an innocent young virgin, yet all the time hot to be deflowered. Then, just as Vivian has squeezed into her tight little nook and the poor violated innocent is gasping and sobbing for breath, pleading with him to treat her virgin cunny gently, in saunters my wicked sister who takes in the situation at a glance, lifts her skirts to straddle the wench's face and forces her ginger muff onto the child's protesting mouth.

"Well, Clara dear, is that what happened? Or am I altogether wrong?"

Clara giggled, amused at the picture of wanton depravity her younger sister had conjured from no more than her own unfettered imaginings.

"Oh, Iris, how you can make me laugh sometimes. The girl was neither of those. Guess again."

"Aha, I think I can guess now. The girl was Rosa, that delicious little maid of Barbara's. Let me try to guess what happened. Vivian and the servant, Jacob, were sharing Rosa's favors upstairs. When you entered the room, she was impaled on Jacob's throbbing black cock, shuddering with her fourth or fifth climax, while Vivian lay on his back and let her soft mouth suck him dry.

"Never one to fail to make the most of such an engaging scene, you then gently detached Vivian's cock from Rosa's mouth and completed the job of sucking him yourself while Rosa's willing tongue busied itself in your voracious cunny."

"Iris, you make it sound so lovely. I do wish that had happened, but, the truth is, I found Vivian asleep amid evidence of Rosa's earlier presence, so I had to make do with his seconds."

Clara then related to her sister exactly what had happened the previous afternoon, describing in explicit detail how she and Vivian had pleased one another. As she concluded her account of her strenuous hour with her cousin, Iris stared at her in unfeigned admiration.

"Clara, you lucky, lucky girl! You actually did all those things with Vivian?"

Clara smiled prettily, then said, "It was all very exciting and thrilling, especially tasting his lovely juice just as I did young George's in Donegal!"

"Was it the same taste, Clara?"

"So far as I can really remember what George tasted like, yes. Though it tasted rather richer, somehow. Remember that George is younger than Vivian."

A hawk dived abruptly in the cerulean blue of the vast sky. Clara and Iris could see Vivian pointing it out to Rosa, the vivacious girl who rode by his side.

Clara half-turned in the saddle to look backwards at Monte, Funchal and the flawless blue-green vastness of the ocean.

"It's as if we are ascending Croaph Patrick in Mayo, just like the barefoot Catholic peasantry."

Iris nodded. "I'm beginning to feel quite as though we are adrift in time in all this rugged grandeur, this antique, passionate, almost biblical beauty. All these fig trees and palm lilies, papyrus-bushes and tree ferns are so very exotic compared to the tame landscapes of Sligo and Roscommon. Look, Clara, Dorothy and Barbara are talking together in a most conspiratorial way. Whatever do you imagine they're talking about?"

"From here it looks as though Barbara is doing most of the talking. Perhaps she's telling Dorothy all about her life before she married her husband. Anyway, I'm sure Dorothy will tell us all about it in the fullness of time, just as she told us about doing those tremendously exciting things she experienced with her father's friends!"

It was as Clara had guessed. Barbara was telling Dorothy of her former life.

"Dorothy, you really can have no idea of just how dreadfully Philistine and provincial life was for me at home in County Tipperary. My family was not really even minor members of the gentry class, like yours, so it was not as though we spent our lives in the saddle or romping with young men at balls. We weren't even Church of Ireland, either; our ancestors were the very dourest kind of Scottish Presbyterians, totally lacking in joy and enthusiasm for anything and everything except prayer and self-righteous good works.

"When I began to express an interest in art at the age of twelve or so, it was as though I'd announced my intention of going on the stage or running away to sea!"

Dorothy and Barbara laughed in chorus at the comparison. Barbara glanced over her shoulder to see who was within earshot. Vivian and Rosa rode together some forty yards behind, Rosa leading the pack mule which carried the party's provisions, while Clara and Iris rode an equal distance behind them, further down the winding track.

"Dorothy, would you believe me if I told you that I was a virgin until I was nearly twenty-three years old? Well, more what the French would call a demi-virgin, if the truth were told."

"One hardly wonders at that, Barbara. What intrigues me is how it came to pass that you were able to go to London and Paris to study art at all rather than how you came to meet Philippe Arouca once you were in Paris."

"Thereby hangs a tale, dear Dorothy. One might

entitle it 'The Odyssey of young Barbara Wyse of Tipperary and how she found happiness.'"

Barbara laughed lightly, furrowed her brow and began.

"Curiously enough, it began with a legacy, just as in the very best fairy tales. An aged great-aunt of mine, whom I'd painted in watercolors and sketched in pastels, died when I was approaching my eighteenth birthday. She left me a considerable sum, to my complete astonishment and delight, on the express condition that I study painting and sculpture in London and Paris. Imagine, Dorothy! An elderly corn-miller's widow decided that I was to study in London and Paris when I had only once been as far from home as Dublin! Well, you can imagine how completely taken aback my parents were on learning of this, can't you? Initially, they were opposed, of course, but the streak of Caledonian avarice got the upper hand once my father had read the terms of the bequest and realized that I had to do as the will said if I were to see any of the money at all.

"So off I went, first to St. Martin's School of Art, and then apprenticed to a sculptress, Marie Vernet, of Paris."

"I'm sure you must have found both cities very agreeable after the dullness and provincialism of life in Tipperary. Tell me, which did you enjoy the more?"

"London was a necessary step before Paris, you know. Paris would have been too great a leap all at once, especially bearing in mind the circles in which I found myself moving."

"Oh, do tell!"

"By the purest accident, I found myself among lesbians, my dear. Of course, I had engaged in the usual little-girl naughtiness at home with one or two other girls of my own age and background, but mixing with graceful and talented young women artists who indulged in what were, to a young girl from the wilds of provincial Ireland, quite outrageous practices, was a different matter altogether.

"Mind you, once I'd begun to drink absinthe and red wine by the liter, let alone begun to smoke hashish, which was quite, quite new to me, I found myself participating with a gusto and flair I would never have dreamed possible!"

"How marvellous it must have been, Barbara. You weren't, I hope, consumed by guilt and self-reproach."

"Oh, at first I was. After a while, though, it all seemed quite natural. Once you've reconciled yourself to the fact that practically everyone you know is doing things which would be regarded with a great deal of disgust and disapproval back in Ireland, even the most depraved acts become quite natural."

"How very exciting this is. What sort of depraved acts?"

"Well, let me give you an example. One radiantly beautiful young girl told me not twenty minutes after we had met that she could think of no greater pleasure than having me sit on her face while she licked me!"

"What was your reaction?"

"I stood rooted to the spot, quite dumbfounded. I must have blushed from my toes to my crown, because the girl laughed in a contemptuous sort of way and said rather curtly that she supposed I was far too much of a coward and a prude to oblige her, even if it meant missing a sublime experience."

Barbara winced at the memory. She remembered the tone of disparagement in the girl's voice as though the conversation had happened only yesterday.

"So what was your response, Barbara?"

"I felt so insulted that I could have slapped her pretty little face then and there, you understand. Fortunately, I controlled my temper as best I could, looked her in the eye, and told her very calmly that I would consider it an honor to sit on her face until she was too tired to move her tongue a millimeter further."

"Bravo!" cried Dorothy, delighted to hear the dramatic twist in Barbara's thrilling account.

"I took my pads, notebooks and loose charcoal sketches off the brass bed in the studio and told her to make herself comfortable while I slipped behind the screen to wriggle out of my petticoats. Fortunately, it was mid-summer, rather than wintertime. Dorothy, you simply can't believe how dreadfully cold Paris can be in the winter months until you've experienced a winter in a practically unheated studio. Where was I in my story?"

"You had told the girl to lie down and make herself comfortable while you went behind the screen," replied Dorothy patiently.

"Oh yes, I remember. While I was behind the screen, I washed myself most carefully. A great deal more carefully than most French women ever wash themselves, I might add. Then I took a pair of scissors and hastily trimmed my bush, something I'd been meaning to do for some time. I stepped out from behind the screen naked from my waist to my feet, my heart pounding away like a steam-engine in my breast.

"The girl, Anne-Marie Villefranche, was sprawled on my bed with quite insufferable nonchalance, just as though she did this sort of thing every day of the week."

"Perhaps she did," interposed Dorothy, eager to hear more about the girl.

"Far from it, my dear. Anne-Marie, whom I came to know very well indeed, was no more a natural sophisticate than I was. In fact, her background was even duller and more stifling than mine, if you can credit such a thing.

"As is the way of provincials showing the world what they can do, though, Anne-Marie more than compensated for her origins. She taught me things I simply would never have believed unless I had witnessed them with my own two eyes.

"What's more, she confided that she had begun to keep a journal, an intimate diary, of her adventures. In the fullness of time, so she said, she will turn the more printable ones into short stories and have them published privately."

"Oh, Barbara, how very thrilling that will be! Please continue your story."

"With as much gentility and composure as I could muster, I clambered onto the bed on which Anne-Marie lay, reached out to grasp the ornate brasswork at its head, and very carefully maneuvered myself until my cleft was poised above her face. Anne-Marie wriggled until her arms were between my thighs, permitting her to stroke and fondle my hips and buttocks, her pert little mouth willing and eager.

"I glanced down and smiled at her, my annoyance quite dissipated. Who, I ask you, could be angry with a girl who had willingly offered to give me pleasure in such a novel way?"

"Did Anne-Marie say anything?"

"Something very short and very, very sweet, Dorothy. She looked up at me, her lovely blue eyes shining, and said quite simply 'I ache for you unbearably, you beauty' and with that she grasped my hips and pulled me boldly down onto her nose and mouth."

"Her nose?" queried Dorothy faintly.

"Oh yes, my dear. What the girl could do with her nose is quite beyond my powers of description. She began to shake her head rapidly from side to side, just as though she was trembling with fever. Every blurred movement brought the tip of her nose into contact with my clitoris.

"I can say without exaggeration that after a minute or two of this I was trembling and so heated with the pleasure she was giving me that I would have felt perfectly warm stark naked in full winter."

"What a pity that the girls aren't close enough to hear you telling this story," breathed Dorothy, her own eyes shining with excitement.

Barbara giggled, glancing around in the saddle once more to look at Clara and Iris riding side by side along the precipitous track.

"The girls will have an exciting treat tonight, my dear. Rosa has promised to show us all her tour de force, her delightful accomplishments as a contortionist, with an even more exciting treat to follow."

"Wonderful!" Dorothy whispered.

"While Anne-Marie was buffeting my glowing jewel with her nose, her hands were softly kneading my buttocks, exciting me until I was quite beside myself with pleasure and practically on fire with lust. My cunt must have been simply running with moisture, a veritable mountain torrent, for I could hear Anne-Marie swallowing at regular intervals.

"Just as my rapture had mounted to my first tremulous, shattering climax, my ardent lover tickled me with her tongue for the first time. Dorothy, you could have heard my howl of delight in China! The amazing thing was that Anne-Marie was nuzzling, kneading and licking me quite calmly while innocent, virginal Barbara was writhing and growling like a woman possessed. Do you believe me?"

"Oh, I do, Barbara, I really do," responded Dorothy softly, remembering the first day of love with her father's friends long ago in Fermanagh.

"Anne-Marie licked and nuzzled tirelessly, careful not to lose so much as a single drop of what she came to call my 'sweet, pearly essence.' I climaxed three times in rapid succession. Each time I reached those mountain peaks of delirious fulfillment she increased the tempo, trying to hold me there as long as possible. At last, though, I could stand it no more. My whole body was shaking as though she had been draining me of my life's blood rather than merely lapping my warm, feminine juices.

"Weakly, my voice trembling like an exhausted child's, I begged her to stop, to let me regain my composure, my very sanity."

"Did she?" enquired Dorothy, aroused and heated from listening to Barbara's thrilling account of her seduction.

"Oh, Dorothy, she wriggled out from between my thighs, pulled me to her and held me fast in a loving embrace, our mouths glued together in passion and erotic heat. The taste of my own juices in Anne-Marie's mouth was altogether too beautiful for words; I can remember that first taste as though it all happened yesterday.

"Of course, later on, when I did the same for Anne-Marie and other women and girls, I came to appreciate that Anne-Marie was right when she insisted that I, Barbara Wyse from Tipperary, tasted very, very good indeed, because some girls and women don't taste good at all, you know."

"Really?" enquired Dorothy, hesitant to exhibit her ignorance alongside Barbara's experience.

"Goodness no, Dorothy. The curious thing is that there's no possible way of guessing how a girl or woman will taste from her appearance. A beautiful countess may well turn out to taste and smell of nothing more exciting than raw squid, while a shy little milliner's apprentice may possess the most exquisite flavor and bouquet.

"As for a girl's ability to climax easily, that's every bit as imponderable.

"Listen, Anne-Marie and I once made love to a Danish diplomat's daughter for practically the whole night before she began to so much as tremble. On the other hand, a maid like Rosa rewards one with a positive Chinese firecracker of orgasms after a minute or two of licking."

Convinced that she had heard enough for the time being concerning Barbara's association with Anne-Marie Villefranche and her friends, Dorothy endeavored to change the subject.

"How did you chance to meet Philippe, my dear?"

"Curiously enough, through a Brazilian opera singer who was Anne-Marie's close companion at the time. I was introduced at a reception at the Brazilian embassy in Paris and it was love at first sight so far as Philippe was concerned. Poor Philippe, so many things had to be kept secret from him until we got to know one another better. Even now, he's something of a prude when it comes to hearing some of the stories my dear friend Anna in Tangier has to tell, although he's quite reconciled to my discreet pleasures."

"Your friend in Tangier? Is she the woman to whom you will give us a letter of introduction?"

"Indeed she is. A more engaging soul and a more interesting person you could hardly hope to meet in the course of a very long life. Happily for her, she is no longer poor, but she meets her living expenses by presenting quite unique spectacles for a discriminating clientele drawn from the foreign community and visitors. Goodness me, Anna has done things nobody in County Tipperary would begin to believe are even possible, let alone likely to be done.

"I gave her almost my entire collection of, well, *toys* of a certain nature. I acquired these toys in Brazil, a country in which such delights are rather more readily available than even in Paris, my dear."

"What kind of toys do you mean?" demanded Dorothy, thoroughly puzzled.

"Toys for one or two people to play with, with or without an audience," Barbara replied mystifyingly.

She smiled broadly before continuing, "In fact, Rosa has brought one along on the expedition so you can see what I mean this very evening."

Dorothy, comprehending at last what Barbara meant, threw back her head and laughed with excited anticipation.

"It will be intriguing to see how Vivian, Iris and Clara respond to Rosa's performance if it is all you imply, Barbara."

Barbara grinned.

"I shall be very surprised if Rosa's display fails to excite those young people quite immoderately, my dear."

THE DELICIOUS DAUGHTER 53-X $4.95

"She shivered a little, turned her face to the other side, closed her eyes and continued to wait. The naked skin of her buttocks twitched spasmodically, but other than that she exhibited no signs of apprehension or distress. She knew that her mother would not come back into her room until the exact moment announced out at the beach. It was usually anywhere from fifteen minutes to half an hour, and the longer delay indicated the offense was extremely serious—as apparently it was this time—for the wait became almost interminable."

THE SLAVES OF CAMEROON 49-1 $4.95

This sordid tale set during the German occupation of Cameroon, is about the women who were used by German officers for salacious profit. These women were forced to become whores for the German army in this African colony. The most perverse forms of erotic gratification are depicted in this unsavory tale!

THE DISCIPLINE OF ODETTE 47-5 $4.95

In turn of the century France, young maidens were threatened with whippings to teach them to protect their virtue. But Odette's family was harsh even for that less enlightened time. Whippings, public humiliation—not even these punishments could keep Odette from Jacques, her lover. She was sure marriage to him would rescue her from her family's "corrections." But, to her horror, she discovered that Jacques, too, had been raised on discipline. She had exchanged her father's harsh hand for the more imaginative corrections of a loving husband. Painful pleasures!

THE KING OF PLEASURE 45-9 $4.95

Stanton Ames has delved deeper into the sexual arts than ordinary men dream of. In his memoirs, he recounts the sexual education administered by his governess, Fraulein Schneider, a devotee of spanking and sado-eroticism. She taught him the resemblance between a whip and a penis and how they can be used together to achieve wondrous delights. Throughout his career in the publishing world, he sought beautiful masochists who longed for the ecstasy and pain he could bring them. Strong stuff!

LUST OF THE COSSACKS 41-6 $4.95

The carriage stopped in front of the house and Vassili, who was first to open the door, bowed his head low in homage to his young master, "Welcome, master," he said humbly. Piotor Kalinnikoff, in his resplendent captain's uniform, smiled and turned to Olga: "You see how I'm thought of here, my beauty," he chuckled. "You'll have more attention here than at the Czar's own court, and the command performances will be much more exciting!"

TURKISH DELIGHTS 40-8 $4.95

During the Allied attack on the Central Powers in Turkey during World War I, the Turks exercised unbelievable sexual sadism against the Greek women guerillas and the English spies who fell into their hands. "With a roar of triumph, Kemil Chokar gripped the girl's whip-streaked breasts and forced her back upon the thick rug on the floor...He went at her like a bull, buffeting her mercilessly, and she groaned...to her own amazement, with ecstasy!

THE TEARS OF THE INQUISITION 34-3 $4.95

"Even now, in mortal terror, Rosanna's nakedness reminded her of her happily married nights. There was a tickling inside her as her nervous system reminded her that she was ready for sex. But before her was a man for whom she could feel only the most deeply rooted horror—the Inquisitor!"

POOR DARLINGS 33-5 $4.95

Here are the impressions and feelings, the excitement and lust, that young women feel when they submit to desire. Not just with male partners—but by their aunts and uncles, their stepfathers and their sorority sisters. Desperate, gasping, scandalous sex!

THE LUSTFUL TURK 28-9 $4.95

In 1814, Emily Bartow's ship was captured by Tunisian pirates. The innocent young bride, just entering the bloom of womanhood, was picked to be held for ransom—but held in the harem of the Dey of Tunis where she was sexually broken in by crazed eunuches, corrupted by lesbian slave girls and then given to the queen as a sexual toy. Turkish lust unleashed!

LISETTE JOYAUX 10-6 $4.75

An innocent maid falls into a nest of lesbians. The four lovely ladies overpower and explore her. They stimulate every opening in her body, sucking her sweet virginal nectar. To their delight, she returns their caresses with a licking lust that exceeds their own. They have awakened a ferocious lesbian appetite. After she marries, the lusty lesbians kidnap the young bride for some more Sapphic savagery. Fiery French perversions!

THE CLASSIC COLLECTION

THE BOUDOIR 85-8 $4.95

Masquerade presents a new edition of the classic Victorian magazine, including several bawdy novels, ribald stories and indecent anecdotes to arouse and delight. Six volumes of this original journal of indiscretion are presented here in all their salacious glory. Good old fashioned smut!

A WEEKEND VISIT 59-9 $4.95

"Dear Jack, Can you come down for a long weekend visit and amuse three lonely females? I am writing at mother's suggestion. Do come!" Fresh from his erotic exploits in *Man with a Maid*, randy Jack is at it again!

TICKLED PINK 58-0 $4.95

A young girl receives her sexual tutelage in a house of torture. From her spyroom, Emily sees her aunt, Lady Lovesport, whip her maid into a frenzy and then tongue-whip her as Mr. Everard enters the bounteous Lovesport's behind. Emily is joined in her spying by young Harry, who practiced the positions he observed. When Lady Lovesport catches them, they became active participants in group sex, with Harry receiving the blows and hungry Emily catching his spunk. An erotic vacation!

THE ENGLISH GOVERNESS 43-2 $4.95

When Lord Lovell's son was expelled from his prep school for masturbation, his father hired a governess to tutor the motherless boy—giving her strict instructions not to spare the rod to break him of his bad habits. But governess Harriet Marwood was addicted to domination. The whip was her loving instrument. With it, she taught young Richard Lovell to use the rod in ways he had never dreamed possible. The downward path to perversion!

A Complete Listing Of MASQUERADE'S EROTIC LIBRARY

THE DELICIOUS DAUGHTER	53-X	$4.95
THE JAZZ AGE	48-3	$4.95
THE SLAVES OF CAMEROON	49-1	$4.95
HOUSES OF JOY	51-3	$4.95
MY LIFE AND LOVES (THE LOST VOLUME)	52-1	$4.95
PASSION IN RIO	54-8	$4.95
RAWHIDE LUST	55-6	$4.95
LUSTY LESSONS	31-9	$4.95
FESTIVAL OF VENUS	37-8	$4.95
INTIMATE PLEASURES	38-6	$4.95
TURKISH DELIGHTS	40-8	$4.95
THE KING OF PLEASURE	45-9	$4.95
JADE EAST	60-2	$4.95
BUSINESS AS USUAL	56-4	$4.95
CHINESE JUSTICE AND OTHER STORIES	57-2	$4.95
A WEEKEND VISIT	59-9	$4.95
TICKLED PINK	58-0	$4.95
KIM'S PASSION	50-5	$4.95
THE EROTIC ADV. OF HARRY TEMPLE	62-9	$4.95
YOUNG ADAM	63-7	$4.95
CLAUDINE	64-5	$4.95
HELEN AND DESIRE	65-3	$4.95
PLEASURE OF PRIVATE EYE	66-1	$4.95
MORE EROTIC ADV. OF HARRY TEMPLE	67-X	$4.95
RED DOG SALOON	68-8	$4.95
MORE PLAYGIRL FANTASIES	69-6	$4.95
NINA FOXTON	70-X	$4.95
DIARY OF AN ANGEL	71-8	$4.95
HAREM SONG	73-4	$4.95
KATY'S AWAKENING	74-2	$4.95
CELESTE	75-0	$4.95
ANGELA	76-9	$4.95
END OF INNOCENCE	77-7	$4.95
DEMON HEAT	79-3	$4.95
TUTORED IN LUST	78-5	$4.95
CLARA	80-7	$4.95
FORBIDDEN DELIGHTS	81-5	$4.95
LUST	82-3	$4.95
SEDUCTIONS	83-1	$4.95
MASQUERADE READER	84-X	$4.95
THE BOUDOIR	85-8	$4.95
JUDITH BOSTON	86-6	$4.95
THE MASQUERADE READER DECEMBER ISSUE		$2.95